"In *Mindset Choices*, Linda Weber speak[...] knowledge and common sense, both o[...]. This book is full of Scripture, which God says, 'will not retu[...]y, but will accomplish what I desire and achieve the purpose for which I sent it.' The biblical passages and the wise principles derived from them have life-changing potential."

> — Randy Alcorn, *New York Times* bestselling author of *Heaven,*
> *The Treasure Principle,* and *Safely Home*

"When you finish reading Mindset Choices you will wonder why someone didn't write a book like this long ago. It is an incredible guide to developing an intimate relationship with God and developing a much-needed Biblical World view. Every Christian should read this and apply the principles of this book in their daily lives. Bless you Linda Weber for stepping up again and writing from you heart in a way that blesses all of us who read this extraordinary book."

> — LTG (RET.) Jerry Boykin, EVP Family Research Council, and
> author of *Strong and Courageous*

"Linda Weber's book is the perfect message for today. So many Christians have lost their joy in this world of compromised truth, but Linda calls us back to our identity in Jesus. I was encouraged and overjoyed to be reminded that I am a child of God and a co-heir with Jesus."

> — Elliette Harrison, wife of Promise Keeper CEO Ken Harrison,
> Bible study leader

"As a former soldier, law enforcement officer, and businessman, I've spent most of my life being taught the importance of having a proper mindset. I've also taught the importance of proper mindset to thousands of others. But, after reading Linda Weber's book, everything that I was taught and everything that I taught others fails in comparison. Linda's book is the best I've ever read on the subject, and it is now a book that I will use and encourage others to use as "the guide" for achieving happiness, success, and a life filled with spiritual direction and wisdom. Linda has captured how to deal with the struggles and hardships of life and how to overcome anything. God will truly bless you if you read, and more importantly, implement the wisdom shared in her book. She is absolutely right: Philippians 4:13, 'I can do all things through Christ who strengthens me.' Thank you, Linda Weber!"

> — Larry G Ledford, president/founder, No Greater Love
> Foundation, Inc.

"With so much loss of hope in this constantly changing world *Mindset Choices* encourages, directs, and guides you on the journey to truly knowing God who made you, formed you, and Who ultimately fulfills you—a must read!"
— Gary and Barbara Rosberg, America's Family Coaches radio
ministry, authors, and speakers

"Linda Weber delivers a strong and vital message of victory. A life of success through the mindset of positivity. Opportunity for growth through difficulties. By refusing to believe the lies of negativity and deciding to imprint the truths of God's character, promises, and provision for our lives. She guides the way to living in abundance verses disparity. We all have difficult challenges, we all have struggles of various kinds, there will always be situations that seem unbearable or insurmountable. Linda provides personal examples of extreme hardships AND she provides solutions.

Whatever situation you may be dealing with, she proves the answers lie throughout the pages of the most critically acclaimed book ever written, the Bible. Linda delivers biblical truths through a multitude of verses written in the Bible to learn, cling too, memorize and keep close to your heart during all life's situations. She lays out page upon page of life truths that can only be found through an intimate relationship with our savior and His word. The comfort and security of choosing the positive mindset is life edifying. Linda proves the Lord's provision for a life of victory by supporting evidence of His word. This is a must read!"
— Dominique Savage, international chef, linguist, artist, Yoga
instructor, Army veteran.

"*Mindset Choices* is an amazing book to read and meditate upon. My strong endorsement of Linda Weber's *Mindset Choices* comes after having been personally challenged and encouraged by it. I feel anyone who reads Linda Weber's *Mindset Choices* will likewise experience its effect upon their lives drawing them closer to God and watching Him work."
— Myrna Alexander, notable author to include *Behold Your God* and
several women's Bible studies. Bible teacher/speaker, international
ministry in Europe, Eastern Europe, and the former Soviet Union
with her husband, the late Hebrew professor Dr. Ralph Alexander,
Israel guide.

"How often do we find a book that is also a gift? One that lifts our spirits and minds and helps others be more prepared to do life meaningfully as we share our insights. Linda has a mature naïveté and childlike faith that packs a powerful, wise, and potent message of God's design for our life and thinking! Using familiar analogies from things like the children's book, *The Little Engine that Could*, and builder's term, 'plumb line,' she maps a true course to God's joy and purpose in our lives. Do not miss this treasure!"

— Linda Campbell, retired school teacher and Bible teacher, with a life in the commercial construction business with husband.

"Linda, you've written a comprehensive, deeply purposeful book for the heart, mind, and soul of anyone willing to 'look in the mirror' and personally plumb the depths of timeless truths needed for evaluation and change measured by the eternal 'plumb line' of GOD'S WORD. You cause the reader to factor in the various influences, such as our culture glorifying the SELF-factor. Readers are challenged to take a hard look at ourselves—our thoughts, motives, and actions; and, then to choose to direct/redirect them to Christ and His truths asking the Holy Spirit to show us where He wants us to make changes and giving us His MINDSET to do it, the God-factor.

Prov 23:7 says, "For as a man thinks within himself, so he is" which rings true as the reader's MINDSET is challenged throughout to evaluate where and on whom their mind is focused self, the world, or God. Admittedly, training/retraining our brain is hard work; but you've done a lot of the homework for us in this book—it's a wonderful resource/manual of sorts filled with so many treasures to use, choose, and FACTOR into our daily personal lives. (I do think it'd be a great Bible Study with a group. I can imagine much discussion happening with lives challenged and changed through the Holy Spirit.)

Finally, I must add that notably gripping throughout were the illustrations and personal stories you shared—each so helpful. The ones that gripped me personally, were examples of your family life, especially those with your incredible mom. Since she (June) lived here in Tyler, TX for many years and went to our church; we grew very close to her and sort of adopted her: she was like another mother to me/grandma to my kids; a personal godly mentor; truly part of our family—sharing many meals in our homes and especially birthday celebrations of our children. Everyone loved June and benefited from her unswerving faith in Christ and His Sovereignty. The God-factored mindset she chose was that God is completely Sovereign, quoting to me and others often in difficult circumstances, "Marilyn, GOD KNOWS." She was also quick to quote, "Trust in the Lord with ALL your heart and lean NOT on your own understanding. In ALL your ways acknowledge Him, and He will direct your path." (Prov. 3:5-6). A true prayer warrior, I concur, as you did in this book, your mom truly epitomized what your entire book encompasses—living a purposeful, directed, overcomer life choosing to have a mind SET on the main thing; and, your mom's MINDSET was JESUS, positive and determined to TRUST CHRIST in ALL—the good, the bad, and the ugly—living a truly God-factored life! May we all, led by the power of the Holy Spirit, choose to abound in hope and do the same! Rom. 15:13, "Now may the God of hope fill you with all joy and peace in believing, that you may abound in hope by the power of the Holy Spirit." YES!

— Marilyn Ackerson, retired school teacher

"Linda Weber's book, *Mindset Choices,* reminds us to set our minds on things above. She walks us through Scripture giving us a vision of what it looks like to guard our thoughts and make godly decisions. This book reminds us that we need to anchor our lives on the truth of God's Word and allow it to combat the lies of the enemy.

"Linda Weber is a woman who loves God and has saturated herself in the truth of His Word. Her guidance for how to shape our mindset and the choices we make flows from a lifetime of seeking God's will for her life, choosing to follow Him through all the challenges, and continually growing in her knowledge of Him. I believe you will find this book a blessing and an encouragement in your spiritual journey."

— Peri Layton, women's ministry director, Good Shepherd
  Community Church

"A few hundred years before the birth of Abram (aka Abraham) in Meso-potamia, Ptah Hotep in Egypt developed the oldest known written guide to living life well. He had lived a long life himself; he began his work at the age of 110! In one of my visits to Egypt, I actually visited the tomb of this ancient sage.

Among his *Maxims* to his son, Ptah Hotep wrote:
"Flood your heart, restrain your mouth,
Then your plans will be among the officials.
Be straight in character before your lord.
Do as he has said, that is the son,
So those who hear it say,
'Indeed, favor gave birth to him.'
Say things of distinction,
so the officials who hear may say,
'How perfect is the issue of his mouth.'"

— Christian Jacq, *The Wisdom
of Ptah-Hotep* (modified slightly)

Ptah Hotep in 2400 BC had the goal of directing proper actions for those who would follow him in the service of a Pharaoh in the royal court. In our modern world, many, from Ben Franklin to Norman Vincent Peale, have instructed others similarly in how to act, how to behave.

Linda Weber, in her book *Mindset Choices: With Vision from Scripture*, seeks to do something deeper. Instead of a focus on behavior alone, Weber presses on one's *mindset*. What it is that leads to an improvement in behavior is based on what one thinks and how one thinks. Her approach is not simply on positive thinking that one strives to achieve, but on the mind itself that is "set" on God.

The late Dr. Earl Radmacher served for many years as the President of Western Seminary in Portland, Oregon, the school where Linda's husband was both student and Assistant to the President. Dr. Earl's passion streamed from Romans 12:2, "And do not be conformed to this world, but be transformed by *the renewing of your mind*, that you may prove what is that good and acceptable and perfect will of God" (NKJV, emphasis added).

The term "mindset" may well be thought of as the divine work of the renewal of one's mind. A truly Christian mindset is more than a desire to be a good advisor to others (as Ptah-Hotep), or a more moral person (as Franklin), or to find power in positive thinking (as Peale).

The Christian mindset is based on a living relationship with God, an ardent study of the Scriptures, and the work of the Holy Spirit in continuous reshaping of how one views self and others. Linda speaks of developing a conscious mindset after our master designer, something that will keep one from disaster and bring more than we ever thought possible. "Why," she asks, "would I want another way?"

—Ronald B. Allen, senior professor, Dallas Theological Seminary

FIDELIS PUBLISHING ®
ISBN: 978-1956454116 / 978-1956454123 (eBook)
Mindset Choices
With Vision from Scripture
© 2023 Linda Weber

Cover Design by Diana Lawrence
Interior Layout Design by Lisa Parnell
Edited by Amanda Varian

Unless otherwise indicated, all Scripture is taken from: New American Standard Bible®, Copyright © 1960, 1971, 1977, 1995, 2020 by The Lockman Foundation. All rights reserved.

Scripture marked (Phillips) is from *The New Testament in Modern English* by J. B. Phillips copyright © 1960, 1972 J. B. Phillips. Administered by The Archbishops' Council of the Church of England. Used by Permission.

Any emphasis in quoted Scripture—whether italics or boldface—is by the author, not the translation.

Order at www.faithfultext.com for a significant discount. Email info@fidelispublishing.com to inquire about bulk purchase discounts.

Fidelis Publishing, LLC Sterling, VA • Nashville, TN fidelispublishing.com

Manufactured in the United States of America

10 9 8 7 6 5 4 3 2 1

Mindset Choices

With Vision from Scripture

Linda Weber

FIDELIS
PUBLISHING

*Dedicated to all you readers who are determined
to incorporate the God-factor into your mindset
for maximum productivity in life. Your enhanced outlook
with Scripture does and will determine your outcome.*

Contents

Mindset Determines
Everything

Let's go straight to our core: mindset needs to begin with the God-factor. As we let Him do an ultrasound of our lives, we escape the numbness of despair and discover what gives purpose. That mindset from choices and decisions we make is only as smart as the information we possess. As we work through these pages together, we'll rehearse a lot of Scripture, giving you tracks to run on. Knowledge of God paves the way for everything as we put it into action, enacting His values. We must indeed pass these values to the next generation. Knowledge is not overrated. (We can take that concept to many arenas of life.)

We all have the continual question, "How do I do life with my present set of circumstances?" Many would say, "But you don't know what I have to live with." Let's work together to find some answers as you discover for yourself how to bring light into what seems like territory too foggy or dark to navigate. If we remain isolated and without the God-factor, we are an accident waiting to happen with the headwinds of life, where the devil is very intelligent getting us to go his way.

We've been born into this labyrinth of life, observing family systems of what is familiar and thus expecting what we saw to be normal. Naturally enough we learn to copy the patterns observed either consciously or subconsciously. We learn to think with these observed patterns, developing a mindset of how to do life. Our consciences start to develop with the way life is done around us. The Bible tells us in Proverbs 23:7, "For as he thinks within himself, so he is."

As we age, the people and training we're exposed to, the relationships and activities we give ourselves to all lend to a likeness we take on. The culture around us portrays a standard to copy and communicates it's offensive if we don't conform. Our mindsets are determined by our presuppositions of what we believe to be true. How do you choose where your authority comes from in defining right from wrong? Are your circumstances pushing you to decide how you respond to everything?

Observing positively influential lives can generate confidence in our spirits to make smart choices with our ongoing question of "how to do life." Regardless how dark things could have been for you, you can choose to be different with a different mindset. You can break loose from the strongholds affecting many. It takes a chosen earnestness to forge ahead through thick and thin. And, regardless of those horrendous past issues, when you are born into the family of God, you have power others don't have. Knowing Jesus and following Him and His intentions for us will change our lives.

Daniel in the Bible was a great example for us (1:8), "Daniel made up his mind that he wouldn't defile himself." Then God in verse 9 grants him "favor and compassion." Oh that we wouldn't defile ourselves with resentments harbored, an unforgiving spirit, being conditional with our love or dominating everything. Many of our self-serving choices defile us, so let's not do it.

The Ultimate Plumb Line

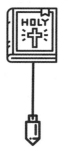

Fortunately for me, I had a mom who placed life's decisions and thinking patterns next to the ULTIMATE PLUMB LINE. I observed this life commitment of what was important and how to handle the hardships at hand. If God said it, she was in, and we learned this firsthand from her. She put her trust in Him and not in our harsh circumstances. What a model for a mindset.

We were created in God's image by our Creator, and He provides for determining the ultimate plumb line—what is right and wrong, and what is best and not appropriate. Our honest consistency of studying our plumb line will drive us to appropriate responses with everything.

This concept demands our allegiance because we are faced with questions everyday of "how do I decide what to do or not?" Back in Genesis, Adam and Eve decided to do things their own way and they put into motion the whole sin nature for all of us. Do we go to our Creator to pursue the ultimate path of light or do we let the self-orientation or dark path prevail? The ultimate plumb line is available and choice is given, so which way will we go with it all? This is of bottom-line importance.

We *choose* our mindset. And there are consequences for going with the direction we choose. So, are we next to the ultimate plumb line? If our passionate decisions don't match His plan, they aren't right. The discussion ends there for the concerned God-follower. To determine honesty, reality, or accuracy of our philosophy of life, we must set it next to the only true Designer of life. Are we dead set with our opposing preferences?

For me, I'm forever grateful the natural tendency to be a basket case when my surroundings were not desirable, to say the least, didn't prevail over my mother's strong influence to have a God-focused mindset.

There were numbers of negatives in my life to overcome. I've moved forty times in my life, and I will say eight moves in the third grade were not conducive for this girl learning how to read. Other things were much worse. My father was an angry, abusive man. He demanded perfection, throwing away any paper I didn't do perfectly. It gets worse. He swore all night at my mom and accused her of everything so unfairly, mostly sexual accusations, which were incredibly far from reality. He threw things that put holes in the sheet rock, put his feet through the wall next to the bed in anger, kicked my mom literally out of bed to hit the floor.

We kids were never allowed to spend the night at other kids' homes as his perverted mind expected bad things would be going on. His selfishness was huge. He didn't work since he thought he deserved more than folks would pay him, so I learned to make things and sell them door to door for spending money for necessities, beginning in the fourth grade. I remember not having soap to wash the clothes or have much to eat.

He would get his guns out at night and talk about killing us, once saying he'd spread our blood from one end of the country to another. He was a sexual pervert requiring us to work to stay away from him because of his continual improper demands physically. I hated getting off the school bus and seeing his car parked at home, because my mom was gone at work and it was scary being around him. He'd take his belt off preparing to beat us with it if we didn't do as he said, and there were beatings. He should have been in jail and us be off to some shelter but those places were not available in that day. Mom did go to counseling and yet either she didn't get thorough enough with her descriptions, or they were afraid to step in and force action that could bring retribution.

After he did leave, when I was a high school sophomore or so, he came back, found us at a friend's house at Christmas, demanded we come with him. He got his gun out of his jacket and told us not to try anything or he'd use it on us. Then, back at our little migrant-type house, during one of his threatening times, his anger raged to the point I saw him hold a wrench over my newborn brother's head talking about crushing his skull if he didn't stop crying. I yelled out, "No, don't do this!" At one point, we learned he hired a migrant worker across the street to kill our mom—fortunately that never happened.

My sister remembers coming home once to find the skin of her pet rabbit hanging on the clothesline. I actually don't remember his barbaric demand after that, but my sister does, making us eat that rabbit. Okay . . . you get the picture. It was a horrible atmosphere, to say the least. It was DYSFUNCTIONAL, AGAINST THE LAW, CODE-PENDENT, etc. You can imagine how we felt it was the best thing that ever happened when he finally left for good. He was a very sad case to say the least and, as I said, should have been taken to jail.

So how do we evaluate all this? How do you overcome such a sick story? I'm told I should be a psychological mess with forever hatred and an inability to ever forgive or function productively. My biological father was a sick man. If likened to a deck of cards, I've said he was missing all the high cards. It seems our mom was afraid for her life if she should cross him or turn him in to police. That wasn't something she ever felt she should do. There are laws against such behavior and she should have pursued the police. With all she gave us in developing our mental and spiritual dependence on God, I haven't been one to be mad at her for dealing differently with our rough life. God did take care of us and we are stronger, trusting Christians for having to face all this.

All to say, we can overcome. We had a mindset that our God is greater than all else. My mother continually rehearsed the character of God, how He knows everything, is all-powerful, is sovereign, is with us, provides, cares, protects, loves us, nothing takes Him by surprise, and He is good. We had a steady diet of learning our Bible at a church, enabling us to know our God. He was and is big enough to meet all our needs. We learned that, believed it, and lived like it was true. Anybody who knew Mom knew she often quoted the verses, Proverbs 3:5–6: "Trust in the LORD with all your heart And do not lean on your own understanding. In all your ways acknowledge Him, And He will make your paths straight." She lived out this trust and passed this message on to thousands.

We didn't complain about what we didn't have. Mom kept blinders on to the negatives of life and pointed us to what was important and good. She'd verbalize how we have everything we need. We two girls have been married to pastors for most of our lives and our brother is a pastor, bringing people to know Jesus, in spite of our harried child-hood. It's interesting how Booker T. Washington said, "Success always leaves footprints."[1]

YOU can overcome too, regardless the difficulties. You can for-give IF you will. And you can avoid the debilitating state of insecurity and enjoy a life of feeling totally secure in who you are. It's interesting and even amazing how many very smart people are quite blinded to their own powers to change things with a proper mindset. Being smart in one realm doesn't automatically transfer to other needed realms for productivity. We'll get into the process needed later, helping you know how and what to do with setbacks and trials for this life of productivity while overcoming whatever. Stay with me. I foresee good things coming for you. (Remember, it's your mindset and the God powers behind you that make a difference.)

Joshua 24:15 says, "Choose for yourselves today whom you will serve." Realize, too, you are empowered—"God has not given us a spirit of timidity, but of power and love and discipline" (2 Tim. 1:7). Then there are terrific results when our mindset is strong—"The steadfast of mind You will keep in perfect peace, Because he trusts in You" (Isa. 26:3).

Life brings much to respond to and we get to choose what our mindset will be to endure and rise above. Are we our own judge, acting like we are God, to prove whatever we think will be best? Or do we choose to go deeper and look to our Creator of life as to how He would want us to choose to pursue life's challenges? Whatever mindset you allow to carry you through life will determine everything on the other side of life's daily choices. What kind of standard will carry you through everything ahead? May we manage these choices earlier rather than later to avoid any propaganda-type world to overwhelm our best interests.

There is so much to learn about what difference our mindsets make. Reading stories and hearing friends tell of petrifying experiences as prisoners of war and others being kidnapped, and then how they escaped or were let go, definitely demonstrate the power of their determined mindsets to enjoy freedoms they once possessed. Extremely difficult circumstances require a positive mindset to get through it all, with a powerful standard. Then there are much lesser pressures demanding a productive process also to rise above it all, but all requiring a mindset to make things happen well.

Meeting with graduates of rigorous training such as the Navy SEALS and Army Rangers illustrates again that they would not finish their demanding training successfully if they were not determined with a positive mindset. (My husband definitely relates personal stories about his getting that Army Ranger Tab, and also his precarious wartime experiences.) Everything difficult requires you to set your mind on the goal and not allow distractions, hardships, unfair treatment, etc. to take you under. You've determined a standard to reach.

Besides overcoming these rigorous experiences with determination, it'll be helpful for us to understand the power of our thoughts and emotions in how they affect our health. This ability to control our minds will make a major difference in advancing our abilities to stay well and away from paths of destruction in numerous ways. Besides our physical health being at risk, we've all noticed how the mental health of thousands has been affected with people quarantined from the pandemic who have lacked coping skills to endure. We don't have to search far to observe the horrible effects of isolation, addictions, and suicides that have soared. Learning to manage our mindsets will strengthen our physical and mental health more than you thought possible.

As you get into the pages of this work, you will relate to many different kinds of situations requiring incredible conscious work for us to be sane on the other side. You will receive tools to develop this mindset as well.

On a less serious level from those examples mentioned above, we observe how our thinking processes affect everything—especially our mindset. Have you noticed how we pursue things we obsessively think about? Before we get into the heart of it all, I'll share a hilarious example of a mindset in the world of our eighty-pound Labrador toddler. He absolutely loves food and even hearing that word causes him to spin out over rugs leaving them in crumpled heaps. He jumps up on all four feet repeatedly, spins circle after circle, dances, whines, and slobbers profusely in pursuit of the food he craves. Funny? Yes. But is what we obsessively think about funny? May it not be in the negative realm.

That one-track mind of our dog reminds me of another story you might relate to. A young pre-teen we know wanted a new bicycle so badly everything that came out of his mouth was hounding his parents to get him this bike. He couldn't think of anything else and drove them crazy until they finally gave in and purchased it, if for no other reason than to just shut him up. Nothing was going to be right until he got what was on his mind. Do we have mindsets?

More seriously, we all get into that one-track mind syndrome in many arenas. If God hasn't been invited into our lives, we have a hole in our heart that lends to filling it with what comes naturally. Then there's the Christian who has allowed disappointments to rule and his mind track reverts to filling up the hurting heart with temporary pleasurable fixes. Only until we heed the Master Designer's plan will we find rest; we do have the choice to follow a mindset or not.

First Peter 1:13–16 spells out what we need to fill that hole. "Prepare your minds for action, keep sober in spirit, fix your hope completely on the grace to be brought to you at the revelation of Jesus Christ. As obedient children, do not be conformed to the former lusts which were yours in your ignorance, but like the Holy One who called you, be holy yourselves also in all your behavior; because it is written: "You shall be holy, for I am holy." (Keep reading that passage for extra credit in life.)

The mindset of emptiness from the hole goes to seed as described in Galatians 5:19–21, "The deeds of the flesh are evident, which are: sexual immorality, impurity, indecent behavior, idolatry, witchcraft, hostilities, strife, jealousy, outbursts of anger, selfish ambition, dissensions, factions, envying, drunkenness, carousing, and things like these."

From emptiness to sadness and hardship, we are going to process together how to develop a mindset to rise above. If you are at the end of your rope having to deal with so much trouble and your feelings being all over the map, you are going to see how feelings are to be ruled and not allowed to rule us when we follow our Designer's life plan. Contrary to what some might tell us, the feelings are real, but we'll discover the better way to overcome.

So much in life is not our idea of a good time. We ruminate over it all. We don't like or want trouble. Injustices abound. Loss of many kinds devastate. There are things we don't have or get to do and it seems like we don't have choices. We don't want to be like elementary children whose immaturity speaks, "This isn't fair; I can't do this; I'll never be happy." Let's go beyond and think about what kind of legacy we are building to leave when we pass. Let's go for that better way together, my friends—stay with me here.

 We're going to have to learn to THINK AHEAD to develop a mindset of positive development in our lives, as it doesn't just happen. It takes skill, work, determination, time spent, and dependence on the Holy Spirit's power. Let's work on this together and not simply say, "Oh whatever." We get to decide.

We may be having to deal with people who have seared consciences and we're left frustrated with how to work with them. It'll be helpful if we gather some understanding of these people so we can know what we're working with. First Timothy 4:1–2 gives us wisdom here, "The Spirit explicitly says that in later times some will fall away from the faith, paying attention to deceitful spirits and teachings of demons, by means of the hypocrisy of liars seared in their own conscience as with a branding iron." (Super strong words, would you say?) Verses 7–8 give us help for our response, "**Discipline yourself** for the purpose of godliness . . . godliness is beneficial for all things, since it holds promise for the present life, and also for the life to come."

That discipline concept requires you to do as was spoken in *The Lion King*, "Remember who you are." For the God-ordained path in life, we remember who we are, chosen by God to be His child and by His power to make life choices after His heart. And, as V. Raymond Edman, the president and chancellor of Wheaton College, spoke from the pulpit at the school, "Never doubt in the dark what God told you in the light."[2]

God gives us confidence if we'll take Him at His word. There will always be hardships and setbacks, which we'll get into later in the book, but we have Scripture to take us through all the steps to survive and thrive. Titus 3:1–11 helps us see we were once foolish with all its downline behaviors and then because of God's love for mankind in saving us—not because of our deeds but according to His mercies—we now have hope. We now have the responsibility to avoid certain things, reject others, and choose to engage profitable things. Having hope gives us the mindset to overcome in the midst of it all.

Vince Lombardi took his football team back to the basics the day after losing a key game, saying, "Gentlemen, this is a football." Our life instruction book, the Bible, takes us back to the basics, among which is having a healthy mindset regarding forgiveness, injustice, and hardship. It's a choice. If God above can forgive all transgressions, who are we to hold others hostage by not forgiving. Are we above what our heavenly Father has done? There is power available to us to be free as we choose to forgive even the tough ones.

- "As far as the east is from the west, So far has He removed our wrongdoings from us" (Ps. 103:12).
- ". . . forgetting what lies behind and reaching forward to what lies ahead, I press on toward the goal for the prize of the upward call of God in Christ Jesus" (Phil. 3:13–14).
- "VENGEANCE IS MINE, I WILL REPAY . . . THE LORD WILL JUDGE HIS PEOPLE. . . . do not throw away your confidence, which has a great reward. For you have need of endurance, so that when you have done the will of God, you may receive what was promised" (Heb. 10:30, 35–36).
- "I can do all things through Him who strengthens me. . . . And my God will supply all your needs according to His riches in glory in Christ Jesus" (Phil. 4:13, 19).
- "With people this is impossible, but with God all things are possible" (Matt. 19:26).

There are obviously different ways to view life's situations but it's going to be smart to learn to view it all through God's glasses for the answers we need.

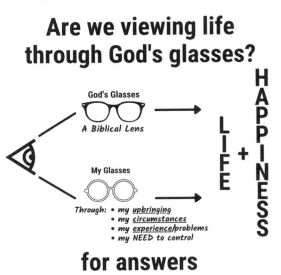

Are we viewing life through God's glasses?

God's Glasses

A Biblical Lens

My Glasses

Through: • my *upbringing*
• my *circumstances*
• my *experience/problems*
• my *NEED to control*

for answers

L
I
F
E
+
H
A
P
P
I
N
E
S
S

The forever question in how our mindset determines everything is to ask ourselves the question, "Are we viewing life through God's glasses?" Are we living beyond the surface view of life?

This is a big question: Are we looking through God's glasses at all? Is there an issue keeping all who view our lives from observing the power in a life lived for the glory of the Creator? Are we providing a stark view for the cause of right for our life observers? Is our mindset such that moves people to pursue honor and justice because of our spiritual strength? Oh, that we have respect for the God-factor and our intentional legacy is left to change lives.

The good news is we get to choose because we are not robots. Our lives can speak volumes as we live beyond our mortal years and realize the enormity of our influence when we have a smart mindset. Go for the gold, my friends, and dwell on this graphic as you evaluate how you are viewing all of life.

Study Questions for Chapter 1: Mindset Determines Everything

1. Thinking biblically, what is one thing that got your attention toward making any necessary changes? Colossians 3:1–3 gives a basic mindset; write it out.

2. How do you work to rule your feelings so they don't rule you? Do you let Scripture help? Write some out. See 1 Peter 1:13–16.

3. Share specifics of how you are aware of your mindset being determined—being influenced by parents, friends, teachers, the Bible?

4. Talk about consciences and how they are developed. See Romans 1:28; 14:19; 1 Timothy 4:1–2.

5. Name some ways you've made decisions that line up with the ultimate plumb line, the Bible. See 2 Timothy 1:13; Romans 15:5; Jeremiah 4:6; Psalm 74:4.

6. Looking at Luke 12:48, how are you fulfilling God's desires with what you've been given? What more might you pursue with how He has wired you?

7. What are some ways people fall away from the faith, changing their mindset? See 1 Timothy 4:1–2.

8. With all God has designed in you, talk about the need for discipline in various realms of your life and how that's related to following through with your mindset.

9. Tell about a time you broke away from a dark side of life when you chose a renewed mindset. Were you listening to God in His Word?

10. How do you define accurate presuppositions? Using Scripture, tell about the foundation you've chosen to build on. See Ephesians 2:20; 1 Timothy 1:4–11; 2 Timothy 2:19; Hebrews 4:12.

11. See Titus 3:1–11. Discuss the hope we have with a mindset God would desire for us.

12. How are you going back to the basics?

13. Discuss seeing life through God's glasses as opposed to seeing through circumstances.

Identify Your Profile:
Look in the Mirror

How you think is how you are. We're going to look in the mirror and observe our profile in this chapter to identify what we're like. Mirrors don't lie, yet the eye of the beholder is a key issue. Proverbs 12:15 says, "The way of a fool is right in his own eyes." Jeremiah 5:21 speaks to this also, "You foolish and senseless people, who have eyes but do not see." May we not be guilty of failing to see as expressed in Mark 8:18, "Having eyes, do you not see?" Spiritual glaucoma is indeed a real problem in too many lives where reality is blocked by that sin condition inferring I'll see what I want to see.

Does it matter? As my father-in-law often said, there is one righteous judge. Second Timothy 4:8 reminds us, "the Lord, the righteous judge, will award to me on that day."

It is amazing how many people are totally blind to their own reality. They may think they are pretty smart with innumerable credentials or money or background, and yet honestly they are missing the reality of what they are like, how people see them. If they could only identify the disconnect causing so much trouble in their lives, they could make progress in positive directions. Let's determine what might be keeping us from being all we want to be. We can't control the people and circumstances around us, but our power is in the responses we choose to make to them. Do we know the difference between good and evil to be enabled to make smart choices through a proper mindset?

Isaiah 5:20–21 says, "Woe to those who call evil good, and good evil; Who substitute darkness for light and light for darkness; Who substitute bitter for sweet and sweet for bitter! Woe to those who are wise in their own eyes And clever in their own sight!"

Are we one of those who waits for everything to fall into place before we can trust God? We say, "As soon as this happens, or something else happens, then we'll trust God, and only then." We wait and wait for things to change. In Habakkuk 3:16–19, the prophet discusses his wait for progress to happen so let's look at his process:

"Decay enters my bones,
And in my place I tremble.
Because I must wait quietly for the day of distress,
For the people to arise who will attack us.
Even if the fig tree does not blossom,
And there is no fruit on the vines,
If the yield of the olive fails
And the fields produce no food,
Even if the flock disappears from the fold,
And there is no cattle in the stalls,
Yet I will triumph in the LORD,
I will rejoice in the God of my salvation.
The Lord GOD is my strength,
And He has made my feet like deer's feet,
And has me walk on my high places."

Are we willing to trust God without waiting for things to change first?

Our personal applications of our chosen belief system will show what kind of mindset we have. It's 2 + 2 = 4. Someone once asked Billy Graham, "If Christianity is valid, why is there so much evil in the world?" To this he replied, "With so much soap, why are there so many dirty people in the world? Christianity, like soap, must be personally applied if it is to make a difference in our lives."[1] So as a tree is known by its fruit, our mindset is displayed by our actions.

It's interesting how we can look in the mirror and see something different from how others see us. We can convince ourselves everything is great when we have some massive blind spots. It's easy for us to notice those lacks in other people. Jeremiah 17:9 says, "The heart is more deceitful than all else and is desperately sick." Also notice in Proverbs 12:15, "The way of a fool is right in his own eyes." Further, Proverbs 16:25 says, "There is a way which seems right to a person, But its end is the way of death." Just what we wanted to hear.

What is MY mindset?

as I look in the mirror

So then, let's identify our profile as we wade through these qualities *slowly* and *honestly*.

Positive Qualities/Actions	Negative Qualities/Actions
Optimist	Pessimist
Unselfish/others-oriented	Self-oriented, narcissist
Grateful	"Poor me"
Forgiving	Harbor resentments
Trust in God	Anxious
Adhere to God's definitions	Redefine all to please me
Pursue God's expectations	Pursue human expectations
Place hope in God	Place hope in self-fulfillment
Build up	Belittle/cut down/find fault
Take personal responsibility	Blame others for whatever
Confident	Fearful
See the good	Bombarded with disappointments
God-conscious	Self-conscious
Open for suggestions	Has to be right all the time
Active, making good choices	Passive, doing what comes naturally

Positive Qualities/Actions	Negative Qualities/Actions
Obedient	Rebellious
Sweet and kind	Sour/unthoughtful
Genuine	Hypocrite
Wholehearted	Halfhearted
Gracious	Arrogant and insisting on own way
Flexible	Stubbornly rebellious
Discreet/cautious	Busy body/out of order
Make the best of	Complain/gripe
Inner strength	Weak fortitude
Pleasant	Obnoxious
Good listener	Have all the answers for everybody
Producing positive fruit:	*Producing negative fruit:*
Love	Unloving
Joy	Miserable
Peace	Hostile
Patience	Impatient
Kindness	Hard and cruel
Goodness	Vicious
Faithfulness	Undependable
Gentleness	Rough
Self-control	Uncontrolled, undisciplined
Steady	Weak
Submissive	Dominating
A developer	A destroyer
Tuned into needs	Clueless of needs of others
Perseverance	Gives up
Hospitable	Closed home for self
Uplifter	Nagger and fault-finder
Heart for God	Heart for self
Seeking peace	Stirring up distrust
Smiler at life	Something is wrong with everything

Producing positive fruit:	*Producing negative fruit:*
Reaching out	Cliquish
Craver of righteousness	Indifferent of God's design
Manage carefully	Manipulate and control
Wise	Unwise
Unconditional	Conditional
Content	Total victim
Grateful	Not thankful
Sacrificial	Takes everything I can get—give me
Tither of finances	Withholder, robber of God
Willing	Unwilling
Diligent	Lazy
Content	Discontent
"Praise be to God"	"God, You've done me wrong"
Reach for the stars	Muddle in the mud of life
Choosing courage	Oh ye of little faith
Life is good	Life is bad
"I can do it"	"I'll never make it"
I have hope in God	I'm doomed, desperate, no good
I have a lifeguard in life	I'm sinking helplessly
Maturity rules in me	Immaturity is obvious
My God is able to handle everything	God isn't capable to handle anything
Waiting on God	"I'll take care of things myself"
Fearless	Scared about everything
"I have all I need"	"Nothing is enough"
Can forgive	Very unforgiving and not forgetting
Build relationships	Separate relationships/deny/destroy
Jump over hurdles	Refuse to try the next hurdle

Producing positive fruit:	*Producing negative fruit:*
Find ways to resolve problems	Insist on being offended and rejected
Work with a problem/find steps	Run away from any resolve
Seek to thrive	Insist on failing again as it's your normal
Believe God and learn more	Insist that God is not there or cares
"I can learn through trials"	"Disappointments always rule in my life"
Not controlled by the dark side	Am codependent and allowing trouble patterns
Display wisdom	Display being the fool as described in Proverbs
Stay strong	Collapse during issues
Call attention to everything right	Call attention to everything wrong
Divert from temptations	Succumb to things that feel good, although wrong
Train mind in Word of Righteousness	"I dwell on what comes natural to my sinful self"
Hold on to my Rock	Depend on good circumstances to carry me
Bestow credit to others	Strip others of credit to feel better
Stand firm	Allow self to be a slave to trouble
Love neighbor as self	Deny neighbor any help
Restore others	Keep taking others down
Assess reality	Remain in La La Land, the unreal
Choose uprightness as defined in Bible	Shame and blame constantly
Have an accurate assessment	Glorify the wrong people
Keep searching the Scriptures	Acquire dust on my Bible, for unawareness
Loyal	Untrustworthy

Model life after God's written word	Follow ungodlike examples/ friends
Listen to the right voices in life	Listen to voices that demean, disrespect or destroy
Advance the gospel	Cause others to stumble in their Christian walk
Know who you are in God's eyes	Allow distraction from "the main thing"
I'm fortunate and am happy	I deserve more, different and better
I'm single minded by God's way	I'm a double minded person, confused
Finding what's right	Finding fault with everything
"God has a plan for me"	"I inherited bad genes and habits from my parents"
I will make it big in life	Nothing ever works for me in life; I'm destined
Regardless of trouble, God is good	I've been violated and it's wrecked my life
Place trust in the almighty God	Place trust in own circumstances
Gracious and kind	Sarcastic and cynical

It's going to take time to wade through these various life qualities so you can carefully put yourself next to them and ask where you really stand. So, taking a good, hard, honest look at your life, to identify your profile helps you understand what people see when they look at you. When you're honest, you'll see where your mindset is; that in turn reflects your life actions.

You may feel you suffer with a ball and chain around your neck from some emotional or physical mistreatment from somebody or some situation in your past. Unfortunately, many feel the need to blame their parents for the way they are. (I heard one parent recently state they are observing this trend to be an epidemic.) And some counselors encourage that practice, so let's be very careful to be fair here. You may not realize how some hardships have unconsciously ushered you into a personal choice of the victimhood pattern. We'll pursue this quality later in this book.

As you have labored through the profiles of the positive qualities and then the negative qualities listed hopefully you've been able to identify yourself in this mirror. Do go slow enough to do justice and think through many situations. Maybe you've been making people around you pay for the internal struggles you've felt in your heart, to get even or justify your pain from holes in your heart. Have you needed to prove your worth? Have you felt you deserved better and thus manipulate others to get it? First Corinthians 13:12 verbalizes our situations, "For now we see in a mirror dimly, but then face to face."

Everything is going to come down to doing this—"casting all your anxiety on Him, because He cares about you" (1 Pet. 5:7). This is our Lord's desire as we look in the mirror, "I pray that the eyes of your heart may be enlightened, so that you will know what is the hope of His calling . . . what is the boundless greatness of His power toward us who believe" (Eph. 1:18–19).

This can be a life-changing experience for you as you get honest.

"Blessed are you who weep now, for you shall laugh" (Luke 6:21).

Study Questions for Chapter 2: Identify Your Profile: Look in the Mirror

1. Looking at Isaiah 5:20–21 discuss how people call evil good and good evil.

2. Being honest, name some times you told God you'd follow His ways as soon as things were going well. Cite examples you've observed. Read Habakkuk 3:16–19 aloud.

3. Discuss ways people are blind to themselves. See 1 Corinthians 13:12.

4. Share how you've chosen to produce Christian fruit from a declared belief system. See Proverbs 11:30. Was it a time you were convicted by the Holy Spirit when reading the Word, or learning from a sermon, or watching a faithful Christian's life?

5. Think together how we need to be honest when evaluating our-selves. What does Scripture say about the heart and the description of a fool? Do a word study.

6. Read together numbers of positive qualities the Bible wants of a God-follower. Stop and discuss as would seem encouraging.

7. Read together numbers of negative qualities and expand how disas-trous they are when allowed. See Proverbs 16:18; 2 Peter 3:16.

8. Ask God to help you incorporate the desirable qualities and to dis-allow all negatives.

9. Discuss the tendency to blame others for our negative traits.

10. Read 1 Peter 5:7 and enjoy together the privilege we have of casting our anxieties on Jesus when dealing with the negatives we observe in the mirror.

11. What is the result as we make smart choices? See Luke 6:21.

Evaluate Carefully:
Ask a Lot of Questions

When evaluating, we must deal with honesty. What is truth and what is falsehood? It is essential we possess information to make accurate assessments, yet how does one decide truth versus errors? We must have discernment, as having knowledge to make these assessments is more than zeal. Romans 10:2 notes this, "they have a zeal for God, but not in accordance with knowledge." It takes work to do research and have knowledge. Hosea 4:6 says, "My people are destroyed for lack of knowledge." Taking this further, 2 Timothy 2:15 says, "Be diligent to present yourself approved to God as a worker who does not need to be ashamed, accurately handling the word of truth."

In our culture we are noticing how many simply decide their own truth, priding themselves on having an open mind. (Are you open to anything?) Consider G. K. Chesterton's comments on an open mind. "The object of opening the mind, as of opening the mouth, is to shut it on something solid."[1] We can't allow ourselves to be "tossed here and there by waves and carried about by every wind of doctrine, by the trickery of people, by craftiness in deceitful scheming" (Eph. 4:14). Discernment is the name of the game.

I'm blown away watching people make declarations of whatever without having a clue what they are talking about. There is much knowledge to be had, research to pursue, and so often, they are severely lacking in the knowledge necessary to make smart decisions. It is sad. It is flat-out dangerous to just be open to anything and follow the crowd. It's a daunting task to pursue details to know how to evaluate important interactions or decisions.

We can't check our brains at the door if we want to be honest. If we say we want something, then there is a prerequisite to adhere to and there are implications. I loved my geometry class (contrary to all in that class) because everything made so much sense. In the practice of math, if this is true, then there are obvious conclusions that follow logic. And this is exactly how it works in life. With a simple illustration, if you want the wrinkles out of your garment, you either get your iron out and iron it or buy a garment with wrinkle-free fabric. If this is true, then here's what must follow. This logic is seen with the following question—DO I WANT GOD'S WILL? If so, there are implications that follow.

If	Then
If I want God's will in my life	Then God is important to me.
If God is important to me	Then His Word is important to me.
	(John 1:1 "In the beginning was the Word, and the Word was with God and the Word was God.")
If His Word is important to me	Then I make sure and get familiar with it daily.
If I am getting familiar with His Word daily	I am aware of qualities and characteristics He would want for me and examples He has provided for me to follow.
If I'm aware of these needed qualities, characteristics	Then I am prepared to make right choices in daily living because I know what they are.
If I'm prepared to make those right choices	Then I am held responsible for those right choices.

"Therefore, to one who knows the right thing to do and does not do it, to him it is sin" (James 4:17).

If we indeed want God's will, we cannot put ourselves in neutral gear. *We must stay in active pursuit.* The passive person won't want to deal with responsibilities or obligations. Don't bother them as they would rather hide or run away from what is needed. They have excuses for everything.

Choosing to stay in neutral gear

Wanting God's will may not be one of your concerns in life. Okay then, let's talk about what gravity is. The dictionary says it's the force of attraction by which terrestrial bodies tend to fall toward the center of the earth. You hold a ball in your hand and let go and what happens? It falls.

The sin factor is a lot like gravity. There is a downward pull that shows itself in the sin nature we're born with. The Bible says in Romans 3:23, "for all have sinned and fall short of the glory of God." We are all born with the sin nature, as started by Adam. "As through one man sin entered into the world, and death through sin, and so death spread to all mankind, because all sinned" (Rom. 5:12). So, like it or not, we're like this arrow going downward, yet—glory be!—we don't have to stay there. Like the truck going faster and faster downhill, and out of control, there can be a change as the driver very specifically turns the wheel to go another direction.

You have to be ready to quickly divert from disaster ahead—like when you see a "WRONG WAY— DO NOT ENTER" sign on a free- way. If you aren't paying attention, the downward trend of disaster will happen immediately if you don't turn the wheel fast to go another direction.

In life, the most important deci- sion we will ever make is acknowl- edging this sin nature we are born

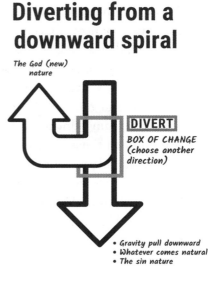

Diverting from a downward spiral

The God (new) nature

DIVERT

BOX OF CHANGE
(choose another direction)

• Gravity pull downward
• Whatever comes natural
• The sin nature

with and choosing to go another direction. Our mindset is going to determine every decision we ever make. As sin is separation from God and choosing to do what comes naturally, the decisions that follow display where your mindset is—pleasing oneself. If you come to the place where you don't want to live on the self-orientation track, and follow the God-ordained plan for life, it's all very different. You DIVERT from that gravity track and make a specific decision to follow the design laid out in the Scriptures. We don't become perfect, for sure. We have a new allegiance and an eternal perspective now. It's a new direction with a new purpose.

Turn hard to change a destructive course

Making this decision will affect everything while having heaven to look forward to. And, with making this decision to pursue the God-design, you have powers He gives you to go through anything. You are not on your own as He is with you; you are born again with a new nature. This gives you the choice of a new mindset, which is a pretty picture. You don't automatically display those negative qualities we saw in the last chapter but have new visions and powers to honor God over self. Lamentations 3:25 says, "The LORD is good to those who await Him, To the person who seeks Him." To avoid the gravity pull and to experience His goodness, notice the responsibility we must enact. If we **wait** and **seek**, then we'll enjoy His goodness.

Probably our largest mindset position is that of trusting. The object of my faith to trust is the key. Is that chair really stable enough for me to sit and not fall? Author Donald Miller says, "The most often repeated commandment in the Bible is 'Do not fear.' It's in there over two hundred times. . . . But fear isn't only a guide to keep us safe; it's also a manipulative emotion that can trick us into living a boring life."[2]

Learning to know God takes a conscious pursuit of spending time in His Scriptures. He will show you what He is like, what He does for you, what He has promised you and what He expects of you to enjoy the results He has in store for you. We will get into this further in a later chapter about the God-factor you are now choosing over self.

The more you give of yourself to this learning process, the more you will enjoy the abundant purpose He has planned for you. The following is a calendar that can give you an idea of why you might be missing some key information about your big God, His design, and how it all works. The black squares could indicate those days of your month when you didn't get around to pursuing your Bible. You were busy and couldn't get to it. If you have numbers of black spots in your month, you can see there's a percentage of your thinking missing key helps for your life.

There's a lot God wants you to know about Him and how you will be most fulfilled. He will show you how to go through your wildernesses and remind you of the powers you now possess as a child of God. I would hope the visual of this month will remind you of how to avoid blank spots in your understanding. We bring upon ourselves deficiencies when we don't show diligence.

Blackened calendar days reveal no exposure to God's word

Evaluation is essential in life. Every good business goes through evaluations. The military, schools, and hospitals are constantly evaluating. In life, we do best when we are smart with our evaluations to identify why and how things are or why they need to get better. It's going to help you learn to understand God's design for everything as you spend time in His Word. You'll see what's happening in our world around us. You'll then figure out what to do with it. It's really the best counseling opportunity you have in putting all the pieces together in assessing your situations. You'll observe dark sides and what to do with them. You'll see light sides and how to follow them for yourself.

You will be motivated to escape the negative traps of downward thinking. You'll be motivated to change negative mindsets by our active will and escape those unfortunate consequences which are bound to destroy our productiveness.

More than anything you will be renewed with an awareness how being next to the heart of God is the secret to everything. You will have wind beneath your wings to trust a big God to give you a meaningful life. Possessing hope through the many trials you face will keep a smile on your face and help those around you to want to find the strength you possess in this hard life.

Even if the people around you are jerks, to put it bluntly, you won't be destroyed. You will have developed a mindset raising you above it all. The devil is like a roaring lion seeking whom he may devour (1 Pet. 5:8). But instead of making excuses for why you can't survive the trouble around you, you will have gained wisdom from your exposure to Scripture, redirecting you from a downward trend of defeat. With careful evaluation, you are prepared to prevent disasters—like Smokey the Bear says, "Only you can prevent forest fires." Only you get to make those moment-by-moment choices leading you to the better way.

In case you need some stimulation in how to evaluate your life, I'll give you some questions to ask yourself. Be honest with your answers.

- What really defines happiness?
- Do I keep seeking things above? (Col. 3:1–2)
- What is really important to me?
- Does it matter how my actions affect other people?
- Do I think ahead to avoid negative consequences?
- Can I see that I've actually set myself up for trouble, or to fail?
- What do I draw attention to?
- Do I get distracted from "the main thing"?
- Am I fooling myself?
- Where do I spend my time, energy, and money?
- Does busyness supersede my Biblical directives?
- Do I have a counterfeit faith with talk and actions?
- Do I get overwhelmed with just everything?
- What kind of impact am I making on those around me—good and bad?
- Is my lifestyle self-oriented?
- Does my mind think after God's intentions?
- What force am I running with?
- Do I have a fixed mindset that doesn't allow God in?
- Do I need to control others to feel better about myself?

- Am I hiding behind whatever?
- Can I hear myself being negative continually?
- Am I consistent or plenty flakey?
- Do I ask "What Would Jesus Do" in most situations?
- Am I trusting God or myself?
- Do I doubt God's Word?
- How do I determine right from wrong?
- Do I shun responsibility?
- Am I owning my poor responses?
- Am I willing to quit my ungodly behavior?
- Who am I serving daily? (you can't serve two masters, Matt. 6:24)
- Am I a "woe is me" person?
- Do I let others into conversations, or is it all me?
- Do I complain about everything?
- Are you displaying the fruits of the spirit: love, joy, peace, patience, kindness, goodness, faithfulness, gentleness, self-control (Gal. 5:22)
- Do you feel desperate and hopeless?
- Are I performance oriented?
- Do I feel the need to correct people a lot?
- Am I thoughtful of other's needs around me?
- Am I trying to change everybody around me? Can I accept them?
- Do I make excuses for everything?
- Do I find myself trying to prove I'm right to others?
- Will I rise above saying, that's just the way I am?
- Do I feel the need to change God's definitions of what's right?
- Do I allow garbage into my brain—TV, books, wrong friends, movies?
- Am I truly unselfish in my relationships, or is it, 'what about me?'
- Do I realize my destructive behaviors?
- Am I continually asking God to strengthen my commitments?
- Do I spot arrogance, narcissism, and entitlement in myself?
- What is keeping me from diverting from Satan's playground?

- Have I figured the only way to be secure is to let go and let God rule?
- How close to God's limits am I pushing?
- How do I decide my priorities?
- Am I breaking God's heart with my waywardness?
- Does God agree with my choices?
- Do I vote according to biblical principles that candidates stand for?
- Have I allowed transformation to take place in my life?
- Is it the breaking of God's principles that makes me angry?
- How do I determine value?
- Am I careful to find my blindspots and correct them?
- Am I aware that trials are used by God to make me strong?
- Am I thoughtful of other's needs around me?
- Why do I feel voids and emptiness at times?
- Am I concerned about the legacy I am leaving?
- What are the strongholds in my life holding me back?
- Am I letting others rent space in my head, to make bad choices?
- Do I succumb to pouting or striking back?
- What am I talking about all the time, what's on my mind?
- Why am I truly secure in Christ?
- Do I let the culture around me dictate my actions?
- Am I silent when I could speak up for what is right?
- Do I know my triggers so I don't go off the rails?
- Do I prepare for expected storms in life by boarding any emotional windows?
- Am I linked strongly with smart like-minded people to ensure the better way?
- Am I searching my heart for weaknesses to strengthen?
- Do I recognize indoctrination into wrong realms and indeed run from that?
- Do I live boldly for my Lord?
- Am I sharing common ground with those who respect God and truth, with God's goals?
- Am I tuned into what demonic influences are so as not to get involved at all?

- Can I recognize fraud when it's present?
- Do I create chaos because that has been familiar in my background?
- Do I go deep into God's Word or stay on the surface?

As I am willing to get honest with myself and answer these questions, I'm prepared to understand my mindset and how it developed. I trust this has been a helpful process to understand your mindset and what difference it makes in everything. Part of the process might be painful but will bring about a better you in the end.

Study Questions for Chapter 3: Evaluate Carefully, Ask a Lot of Questions

1. Read aloud the "If /Then" cause-and-effect progressions. Discuss your responses.

2. Share any seasons when you've found yourself in neutral gear. (Optional)

3. Read Romans 3:23 and rehearse what this downward trend is like in life.

4. Explain what must happen to get off the gravity flow pull. What word encouraged you to remember the action necessary? See 1 Peter 3:11.

5. What two verbs show our responsibility to avoid the gravity pull as we read Lamentations 3:25? What is the result?

6. Discuss the calendar with the blackened days showing our lack of a God pursuit in the Scriptures. Tell how this helps you grasp your lack of understanding.

7. Why do we need to be aware of the difference it makes when we avoid Bible reading? See 1 Peter 5:8.

8. What is an important question you must ask yourself as you read Colossians 3:1–2?

9. Take some time to slowly read some of the questions offered in the chapter to get yourself honest with your God pursuit.

10. Read James 4:17. How serious are you about learning what the right things to do are? What is the result if you don't follow through?

Positive Voices
for Positive Return

There's nothing better than hanging around people who look for the positive in everything. They are productive and seek excellence in whatever realm they are moving. It's refreshing and motivating to want to ride this wave of hard work to produce quality. There's power and strength in seeing their determination find success and purpose, which then motivates you to go and do likewise. You'll need a diligent mindset to actively pursue finding these positive people and opportunities.

In real life you find yourself in all kinds of uncomfortably dark situations, so you need to run to the positive people we just described. And you need the positive voice of the Creator of the universe whispering in your ear. (We discover that in our Bibles.) You can name hundreds of those dark times, yet, with Jesus, there are reasons for everything, a foundation to rest on, purpose to claim, and stability to apprehend. There's hope and acceptance. Psalm 18:28–30 reminds us, "For You light my lamp; The Lord my God illumines my darkness. . . . He is a shield to all who take refuge in Him." His positive voice gives you confidence with everything. There's no need for running away, allowing anger or choosing disillusionment. Don't let the "noise" of wrong influences keep you from listening to God's advice.

Whatever level of desperation in which you find yourself, you need the internal fortitude and confidence to hear the voice of the Lord. (Hear it and do it.) So when you are in strained relationships, inequities, loss, betrayals, and unfairness, God is near to whisper His help. Second Peter 2:9 says, "The Lord knows how to rescue the godly." He's on your side and will help you with His reassuring voice to deal with the powers of darkness. Remember, Ecclesiastes 2:13–14 says, "Then I saw that wisdom excels foolishness as light excels darkness. . . . the fool walks in darkness." No falling apart.

Sometimes voices ringing in our ears are those of our parents as we grow up. A friend relayed a story to us of how a young child lived out the positive voices of his family, even in his hardship of being a Down's syndrome boy. This young man accepted what he was given and made the most of it as he walked in the confidence he continually received from his parents. The father was a university professor at an Ivy League school and could use thousands of words a day. But his son in his disabled body had about 300 words, and he used all 300 for the glory of God on a daily basis—contrary to how the dad said he himself didn't use all he'd been given in life on a regular basis.

This dad was very proud of this son, and even more so than his other kids who didn't use their life gifts to capacity. This special-needs son maximized all he was given because of positive voices reminding him he was worthy of an important life. He felt accepted and was out there being all he could be.

Oh how important it is to choose carefully the people with whom we spend time. There will be influence there, one way or another. Your attitudes and patterns along with life patterns are formed. Consider this word from Isaac Newton, "If I have seen further it is by standing on the shoulders of giants."[1] Are we choosing to stand with giants? You'd better find them because the tendency to bail out when things get tough is all too common.

As a child, many of you read the little Golden Book titled, *The Little Engine That Could*. She was a happy little train so full of joy to bring good things to the children. She had such a bubbly spirit and then, all of a sudden, she stopped with a jerk. She couldn't proceed as the wheels wouldn't work. When the little train tried to get help from a bigger train with what they thought had a more important load, the little engine was told, "Pull the likes of you?" The little train begged for help but to no avail, but she didn't let that get her down.

A famous female tennis player's husband credits his mom and dad for creating in him a mindset to always "show up" when his wife was so busy with her demanding life. He knew it was an uphill battle to get quality time with her, but he was trained to make the most of the opportunities he had to be with his wife. The mindset they instilled created a passion to make good things happen.

What mental voices do we have embedded to carry us through challenging times, and then what kind of responses are we prepared to make? Things just aren't going well, and we feel stuck. Nobody seems to care. Nobody seems to be available to help or are interested in trying to help. We feel so defeated by our situation. So we try plan B and ask somebody else for help to get on with things. Same thing—people around us have many reasons why it won't work with their schedule and they refuse to help.

That reminds me of a trip I took alone to Singapore to visit a dear friend. I had just come out of rotator cuff surgery and was in the recovery stage, wearing a complicated sling to aid my healing. When it came time to put my carry-on suitcase up in the bin above my seat, I asked a strong young man if he'd be willing to help me and get my bag up there to the bin.

Wow, he actually told me no, and just looked away to read his book. *Okay, I'll just ask somebody else*, I told myself. There will always be people like that. So I asked another young man if he would help me get my bag in the overhead bin. Again, I was told no. He just didn't want to. *Really?* I simply needed to proceed to plan C.

It's interesting how it was a middle aged and a more unlikely looking gentleman who was my third person to ask and he was totally happy to perform this rather easy job for me. *Thank You, Lord, it's working now.* It was necessary to not quit and keep trying. My getting mad or defeated or giving up was not an option for making things happen. It was necessary to have that positive voice inside me saying, *I know I can get this to happen.*

I know two coaches who each ended up losing one of their star players to freak accidents and death. What devastating times for any family or coach to have this happen. The close people to these young men who died lament over their passing and then try to work at finding the best response possible; we're all different how we handle loss. It is a long subject to cover in how one responds to loss. One coach spoke and acted with kind compassion. And he knew his attitude about it all would help his players learn to respond to hard things, making the most of how they were going to get through this. The other coach felt so "blown away" that his depression led him to quit his coaching career because he just couldn't handle such destruction of lives. The positive voices inside us need to prevail during hard times so the result is productive.

Back to the little train, the second train she asked to help repeated three times, "I cannot. I cannot. I cannot." He was determined there was no way. Then, the third train that came by the stranded little train said, "I'm not very big." But after hearing the story of the need at hand, the third train said, "I think I can. I think I can. I think I can." She tugged and pulled again and again and slowly it started to move. This little savior train again repeated those words five more times, "*I think I can.*" Oh my, happiness prevailed as the two little trains went up, up, up, and faster and faster and faster. The little helper train seemed to say as she puffed steadily down the mountain, "I thought I could. I thought I could. I thought I could. I thought I could. I thought I could."[2] Are we like that train? We need to be.

What thought processes do you think David was allowing when he faced the giant Goliath and his strength? He went into that experience focused on God's strength behind him and not the physical abilities of the giant. We must face our giants in the same way. *I know I can, I know I can. I can do this because I'm depending on my big God.*

What an example to us of our positive **thoughts** turning into positive **feelings**, turning into positive **actions** and then positive **results**. We can take this to real life and let it repeat with situations we face every day.

Your positive life outlook can change impossibilities into victories, disasters into triumphs, and inward inspiration can actually control your outcomes. A positive spirit enables better health and a powerful life to change everything. Why wouldn't we?

It's possible a course you desired, worked hard toward, and were actually good at might have completely changed into a different direction. Things end up working well into a different path than you ever put together as a possibility. Your mindset will help you as you allow changes and differences to be a positive part of your new package. We don't have crystal balls but opportunities to adjust gracefully.

Positive development

POSITIVE THOUGHTS
↳ POSITIVE FEELINGS
  ↳ POSITIVE BEHAVIORS
   ↳ POSITIVE RESULTS

Jesus speaks to us about everything. In John 16:33 He says, "In the world you have tribulation, but take courage; I have overcome the world." Let's allow those words to ring in our heads, knowing Jesus has gone before us to help us through. Count on it.

There's a song I love to sing over time, "God Will Make a Way."[3] It has ministered to my heart in times of need and it needs to be our subconscious attitude in the middle of all those tough situations we find ourselves in. You can be the fulfillment of your own prophecy when you tell yourself you can do this or that and the power of suggestion comes true. Along these lines, spending time with the right crowd of people will make a difference, as they are supporting your positive outlook choice. Our mindsets rub off on each other.

The Bible gives us examples of prominent leaders needing to listen to positive voices. Isn't it interesting how Moses told God, "Who am I, that I should go to Pharaoh, and that I should bring the sons of Israel out of Egypt?'" (Exod. 3:11). God reassures Moses, "Certainly I will be with you, and this shall be the sign to you that it is I who have sent you" (v. 12). God continues with his reassurance to Moses' insecurity of negative feelings, "who has made man's mouth? Or who makes him mute or deaf, or seeing or blind? Is it not I, the Lord? Now then go, and I, even I, will be with your mouth, and teach you what you are to say" (Exod. 4:11–12).

In Judges 6 we see Gideon being insecure and needing God's positive voice to motivate him. God gives him the positive reminders, "Go in this strength of yours and save Israel from the hand of Midian. Have I not sent you?" (v. 14). Gideon isn't thinking positively. He responds, "Oh Lord, how am I to save Israel? Behold, my family is the least in Manasseh, and I am the youngest in my father's house" (v. 15).

God shows His patience and reassures him, "I will certainly be with you, and you shall defeat Midian as one man. . . . I will remain until you return" (vv. 16, 18). God gives us reminders through His positive voice to reassure us of His intense work in our lives.

We see these reminders with other biblical characters. Jeremiah tells God, "I do not know how to speak, Because I am a youth" (1:6). God reminds Jeremiah with the same kind of message He told others, "Do not be afraid, of them, For I am with you to save you. . . . Behold I have put My words in your mouth" (1:8–9). Those positive voices to biblical characters need to resonate with us today as well.

Watching others who have learned good patterns to live by reminds us that a positive attitude will help us too. The voice *I can do this* inspires us toward greater results. As a man who was trusting God, Christian speaker Nick Vujicic got up before many thousands at the Promise Keepers gathering in Dallas, Texas, and spoke powerfully of God's good work in his life. This man has a positive and grateful attitude, and he literally has NO ARMS OR LEGS. How could anyone in that state of affairs manage to have a positive outlook on life? Sometimes it can help us when we see somebody in much worse situations to see they have overcome and so can we.

You may have heard of the brand Life is Good. That line developed because a mom provided continual positive voices to her six kids around the dinner table. Even though the dad and mom were in a serious life-threatening car accident and things were pretty tough, Mom was always encouraging each kid to tell what was good about their day to the rest of the family every night. That practice of rehearsing positive stories stimulated the two teenage boys to start a T-shirt business, making some needed money. They put Life is Good on each T-shirt in different settings. It grew to a 100-million-dollar business and has advanced many other products. That's a strong story of a mom who demonstrated what difference it makes to have positive voices in their lives.[4]

Our three sons played high school basketball under Coach Tom Johnson, who knew how to take average talent to the top of the state with their wins. He knew the power of encouraging words, so he would gather his teams into a circle after practice and had each player tell what they appreciated about each player. How invigorating for them to feel like they were something special and then take that confidence into how they played the game and how they did life. Positive voices take you to the high ground.

You may remember that Kenny Rogers song, "She Believes in Me." Your motivation to reach for the stars is maximized when you hang around people who believe in you. They see your heart and abilities and they tell you. They help you believe in yourself more than you might have been willing to do on your own. Your motivation is enhanced and you work to live up to this beautiful vision they have of you. You can surprise yourself and even others who previously chose only to see your weaknesses. So who are we going to listen to?

In psychology you learn how Pavlov's dogs showed how food is an unconditional stimulus and salivation is an unconditional response. (This is quite true with our Sky dog.) In life, when we have people around us complimenting us on the good things about us, we are raised to higher levels of confidence. They are not so worried about what might not be our strengths or how we don't do everything perfectly. They see our potential and we even try harder to be more of the same and greater. Reinforcement stimulates response and motivation. I might add, we don't have to have a high IQ; we just need to be determined to allow a mindset of the positive to rule our life. Put yourself in situations where that positive option will be present.

Yes, listening to the right people to give us a good perspective is good, and God uses people in our lives to speak His message in word and deeds. Yet getting our perspective from the God who created and designed us is the ultimate Person to listen to. We'll get into the God-factor in a later chapter, which is the bottom-line answer to everything. He who could part the Red Sea for deliverance can surely take us through whatever we face in life. It's our choice to stay positive about it all; He's with us and will grant us the freedom of positivity, as we earn it.

In my home of origin, it was an ongoing habit for our mom to keep a steady stream of positive talk going, especially in the midst of the traumas present in our home. We took those positive rehearsals of how our God was good, being all we needed to our adult lives. It was not a focus that we had no money or many belongings or a nice house or whatever. That didn't matter. What we had was enough and we had a lot to be grateful for.

Although we couldn't afford to just go out and buy a new tennis racket when I decided to learn, I acquired an antique version of a racket that still had strings in it when one of my grandfathers died. I took that thing out and beat balls against a next-door warehouse wall enough to develop the necessary proficiency to make the high school team, even at the late age of sixteen. That started a life pursuit of the game for me. Later I got my sons going with the sport, watching them achieve rather high levels in high school and college, including a national ranking. Kent went on to be a tennis pro in New York and Ohio for a season. The positive voices of just being grateful when I "happened onto" that old racket gave us a great start and did us well in the midst of not being able to just go buy what I'd like.

So, I took that "normal response" into adulthood. I was grateful I had the opportunity of growing up with positive voices from Mom to frame my experiences—not everyone shares that same heritage. As an Army wife, we arrived in Germany shortly before I miscarried our first pregnancy. I had to go through that unfortunate experience when my husband was away on maneuvers, while not knowing anyone in this new country, city, or officers' quarters building. I was whisked off to an Army hospital thirty-five miles away to endure that loss alone. I've always just gone with the saying, "you do what you gotta do" and did not allow myself to freak out over hardship. It's the way it is and I can make it.

With no cell phones and my husband's top-secret clearance, he was obligated to stay home by the phone almost all the time when not in his office. We weren't able to go together into the little town where we lived for months. So when his superior called him in and told him he could take a week leave, we were excited to go exploring. We only had ninety dollars to make that happen, so seeing Austria, Italy, and Switzerland was done on what you could say was a very low budget. But we saw all those places and we were grateful.

Those little voices we'd hear told us we were fortunate, even though we had to sleep in the car while I was pregnant, and we couldn't afford to enjoy a plate of spaghetti in an Italian restaurant. I went back years later and got my real spaghetti. Those romantic and cute gondolas in Venice would have been fun to experience, but I was happy enough to get to be there and ride the big group taxi boat. That $90 figure also had to cover frequent road tolls and film for my camera. Those who know me would know that was tough because of my desire to take a lot of photos.

Some months later I gave birth to our son, Kent, in the same hospital where I experienced such loss. Having our son join our family was an ecstatic time, yet the hospital process there was not a pleasant experience. All the other army wives were complaining severely with how we were cared for, as they didn't happen to have the privilege of growing up with positive voices to remind them they could do this. There were many details I could relay that would make you cringe, but again, I was prepped to respond with gratitude instead. It's the better way.

Beside the nine different duty locations for our Army time, there was a whole year I cared for our infant son without my husband when he went to Viet Nam. There was no e-mail, or texting or cell phones to connect. The few times we talked were through a radio operator as we'd say "over" after each sentence. Many of the Army wives did not have positive voices in their heads to deal with hardships like this or anything else. Many did not stay married.

It was our desire that our first two children be not more than two years apart if possible. This required that I get pregnant during our only five-day R and R visit in the middle of that Viet Nam year. Bingo and thank you Lord. So, Stu comes home after that war time and I'm five months pregnant.

Then we started seminary toward a life in ministry. We started with two little boys and finished with three. I really don't know how we had anything to eat since there was no money to work with. One farmer in the church would fill my car, floor to ceiling, back to front, with his leftover veggies from his farm. I learned to eat cauliflower—as there was lots of it. Foodwise, people gave us smelt to eat. I did eat it as it was food, but I won't be partaking of that oily fish again. I didn't see downtown Portland for two years because we didn't have gas money to take off and even see the city we lived in. Hardships were plentiful, but we did have a vision that we were there with a purpose so we could deal with anything. It was challenging.

During this bleak four-year season of seminary, God put miraculous pieces together so that we could study in Israel for nine weeks, with a three- and five-year-old at home. That is totally an out-of-the-box God thing in our lives. My husband, Stu, felt it was important to experience the country to color his teaching over the years. Positive voices said this could happen and it did, even though it was a bare-bones experience. Even back then, $1,300 per person was not much to cover round-trip airfare, food, lodging, and entrance fees to exhibits for nine weeks. But we did it. Stu lost twenty-three pounds that summer but we were there with a purpose, so our attitude was positive.

Many people contributed money toward this trip, and miraculously Stu's parents agreed to move into our home from out of town and care for our two little boys for those nine weeks. It was all a God thing, with positive voices saying, *I know we can do it.*

God prepares us for so many things in life. I was used to no money to live on and Stu's next job only paid $8,000 a year as an assistant to the president at the seminary. Interestingly enough after four years there we then were involved in starting a church, which was God's plan all along. Would you believe, once again, we only received $8,000 a year and with three children to support. Those positive voices ruled for both of us and that determined everything. We had our sights set on the mission we were called to. For years it didn't increase very much, so when our oldest was graduating from high school and hoped for an electric razor as a gift, I had to tell him we'd like to get that for him but we simply didn't have the money. The point is we chose not to be distracted; instead, we maintained the mindset God called us to.

So how do you put three boys through college at a private Christian liberal arts college 2,000 miles away when you are basically dirt poor?

We're still not sure how God put all those pieces together, but each of them graduated from Wheaton College debt free. This is where your faith becomes sight. When you know something is supposed to happen, you depend on a big God and work hard to do your part. There's no quitting along the way.

One of those many pieces was this. When it was getting close for our oldest, Kent, to go to college, the phone rang and it was a father of one of Stu's roommates from Wheaton many years ago. We hadn't seen this gentleman in fifteen years. He said, "Isn't it about time your son is to go to college?" To our incredible amazement, he said he wanted to make that possible. Really?! Does this kind of thing really happen? We didn't know how much that would be. Sure enough, for each of the three boys, he sent money to the school and it was just the amount needed after all their scholarships, aid, summer job money, and money we could come up with. *Thank You, Lord, big time.*

At one point when we had two there at the same time, it was appearing we were so far from making it all work that we prepared Blake to come back home for a while to a less expensive school while Kent finished up. We were three weeks from the time they would board the airplane and leave for school, with the return tickets purchased earlier, when the phone rang. It was a friend of Blake's who was inquiring about how it was going. He told her it looked like he was going to have to find a less expensive school around home for a while as we were financially short. She then asked, "Well, how short are you?" He told her we were $10,000 short. We knew we couldn't borrow it because we didn't have the income to pay it back. Without a hesitation, and without talking to her father, she said, "Daddy will have a check in the mail tomorrow."

Oh my, did we ever drop to our knees and cry! How could this be? We've never met her father. He doesn't know us. How could this happen? Blake answered with, "It looks like God is speaking quite plainly that I get to return." I tell these stories because they were real and point to our God's provision "from the sky," so to speak. We give Him honor as He used His people to be so generous and for all of us to be helpful to others.

We need to think positively, and let the voices of, "I know I can, I know I can, I know I can" continue and watch God work. He is big and cannot be limited. No quitting allowed.

You can craft your mindset by gaining wisdom and then acting on it. There is a power of positive thinking; it doesn't just come naturally.

- You can be resilient if you WILL.
- You can make changes if you WILL.
- You can thrive through difficulty, if you WILL.
- You can be content when things aren't all that nice, if you WILL.

Our mental state is going to display what our spiritual health is. (Your physical state is going to reflect it all too.) Think about that. My choices to be and to do come from somewhere, and a good mental state can encourage a longer physical life and with better health, as well.

You *can overcome*, yet it won't happen if you feel the need to compare yourself to everyone. You get to *set your compass* as to whether bitterness and an unforgiving spirit over wrongdoing prevails or not. You *can choose to find satisfaction in building relationships* as opposed to rejecting people. Do stop and think about that.

In the process, a sweet accepting spirit will set you free to live and display a God-honoring life. You'll feel abundance as opposed to choosing a violation mindset. And it will multiply as others observe this uplifting force in you. Everything is going to be okay, if you choose your "heart security" TO LET IT BE. Are you catching this concept? This is serious. IF you choose to NOT hold hostage those who have done you wrong by *forgiving*, **you and they will be free to enjoy life**. You and relationships around you will become whole. Why let the typical dysfunctional patterns around us be a factor in our lives? Why allow destruction to prevail in your family and friends? Mindset shows—is it pretty or does it need some work? Do stop and ponder this at length. Choose to be a winner.

At one point in our lives, my husband was experiencing some unknown pains from a Viet Nam parachute accident. The doctor was perplexed and at one point thought it could be ALS. That diagnosis would be a debilitating death sentence. One friend said, "What's the worst that could happen?" (That was sensitive . . .) And it was obvious: Stu would die and go to heaven. So the friend then said, "And that's the worst?" It did require a positive mindset.

Okay, so we have setbacks and trials along our paths in life, and we'll get to that chapter in this book. But let's keep looking at some positive thinking. Where there is a will, there is a way, I've always said. Growing up, I had no options for babysitting in my neighborhood when I really needed some money, so I looked for other options and they worked. I was determined not to be overcome with defeat but instead to overcome. I guess that's how I was chosen "most determined" by my high school class upon graduation.

Developing a positive trend in your life from positive interior voices speaking to you will require your being flexible and responsible. As you learn to go with the flow more, you'll reduce your stress levels. That song, "Whatever Will Be Will Be"[4] can play over in your mind. Your biggest factor for enjoying positive trends will be listening to God. Whatever He has said in His Word about you, prepares you to know who you are and how to proceed with everything.

For me, I sang songs to my kids that reflected the positive way I hoped they would respond—"My Lord Knows the Way Through the Wilderness"[5] and "Because He Lives, I Can Face Tomorrow."[6] And, one of my favorites, "Be Thankful For the Good Things That You've Got."[7] You'll also love this reminder "Dig Another Well."[8] When studying the effects of music on the brain you will discover many people of note reinforcing positive behavior development. It is impressive to observe how music impacts brain function and thus behavior.

With all this talk about listening to positive voices so as to enjoy the positive return, let's discuss how important it is to pass this life pattern down to the generations in our homes and to those watching within our sphere. Parents possess the privilege and responsibility of helping form the wet cement of our children's thinking and follow-through actions. Parents teach how to respond in life to everything and display attitudes to mimic. The younger generations have voices speaking in their minds of how to proceed with life choices from watching us.

We are prepping these observers to think they will make it in life or not, through it all. What are those voices speaking to these young ones?

Is it to be fearful, angry, and hostile about everything, or are they learn-ing hope and gratefulness as they incorporate the traits from our master designer, the Lord God. Are they learning to forgive and be stable? Or, might they be taught to claim victimhood in the midst of issues? We get to decide what they see and hear.

Rehearsing Psalm 139:13–18 teaches us all to think positively about who we are. It keeps us from getting sidetracked.

> For You created my innermost parts;
> You wove me in my mother's womb.
> I will give thanks to You because I am awesomely and
> wonderfully made;
> Wonderful are Your works,
> And my soul knows it very well.
> My frame was not hidden from You,
> When I was made in secret,
> And skillfully formed in the depths of the earth;
> Your eyes have seen my formless substance;
> And in Your book were written
> All the days that were ordained for me,
> When as yet there was not one of them.
> How precious also are Your thoughts for me, God!
> How vast is the sum of them!
> Were I to count them, they would outnumber the sand.
> When I awake, I am still with You.

Make sure you hardwire these words into your heart.

Study Questions for Chapter 4: Positive Voices and Trends Around Us

1. Share a story from your life when a positive voice inside you reminded you that you could accomplish some hard task. Read aloud Philippians 4:8–9.

2. What Scriptures come to mind that will keep you from utter defeat when hard things happen? See 2 Peter 1:19.

3. Make up a situation where the progression of your **thoughts** to your **feelings** to your **actions** to the **results** would make you feel victorious in life.

4. Look up John 16:33. Do we have trouble in life? What verb shows what we are to do? How does victory take place? How often do we let this progression take place? Admit your answers.

5. What positive voices did God provide for Moses when he was being negative (Exod. 3:12)? What did God tell Gideon (Judg. 6:14, 18) when he was insecure? Look at the positive voices God provided Jeremiah in his doubting. See Jeremiah 1:8–9.

6. Name some people you have watched who provided a positive example and voice of reminder to respond smartly in life.

7. What illustrations from this chapter encourage you in following after positive voices and examples?

8. Share how you are newly motivated to follow positive voices or provide positive voices for others to follow.

9. Rehearse out loud the blessings of our God, how He designed you with much purpose. See Psalms 139:13–18.

10. How will the story of *The Little Engine That Could* remind you to respond in life?

5

Negative Voices Bring
Negative Consequences

"A lie doesn't become truth, wrong doesn't become right, and evil doesn't become good, just because it's accepted by a majority," said Booker T. Washington.[1] We must remember this when we are bombarded by negative voices all around.

"It doesn't matter." How many times have we heard this voice in our head when we're deciding to partake in something totally questionable? Maybe it's our friends who remind us to just go ahead and do it when we know better. This trend started in the garden of Eden. God told Adam, "From any tree of the garden you may eat freely; but from the tree of the knowledge of good and evil you shall not eat, for on the day that you eat from it you will certainly die" (Gen. 2:16–17).

The devil came along and tempted Eve telling her it didn't matter. Then, as she "saw that the tree was good for food, and that it was a delight to the eyes, and the tree was desirable to make one wise, she took from its fruit and ate; and she gave also to her husband with her, and he ate" (3:6). Oh my, it *did* matter—that started a lot of trouble for all of us downline, and the Lord spells out consequences. How many times do we go with the lie, "it won't matter," if I do thus and such? Deception by the father of lies, the devil, is a major problem in our lives.

The Bible warns us about false teachers out to deceive us. There's a lot of talk today about misinformation, and how by it, we are tricked into considering all kinds of culturally accepted living patterns firmly warned against in the Bible to be anti-God. When things become so common around us as normal, we are deceived into thinking it's no big deal to be like the culture around us.

We all stand before the Lord God to demonstrate our loyalty to His divine plan and intentions while firmly rejecting with confidence the devil's desire for us to do whatever feels good to us. Jesus will be evaluating us so we must be prepared. Jesus was angry about sin. He didn't have compassion for sin—it's black and white. Ephesians 4:25–27 tells us, "Speak truth . . . Be angry and yet do not sin; do not give the devil an opportunity." He had compassion for the sinner and encouraged them to follow Him; He showed grace and truth. We need to proceed after the Lord God's example, as unpopular as it is to not follow those negative temptations.

Negative voices whisper that we aren't happy, and it usually feels like it's somebody else's fault. That somebody else so often is someone close to us. Our anxiety causes us to see the glass to be half empty and not half full. We can hear those folks around us, how nothing is ever right. These whispers of negativism find something wrong with everything. They see no good with those around them. The sky is falling and there is a burr in their saddle. Frankly, they make life miserable for everybody around them.

The people we spend time with make such a difference. Proverbs 13:20 reminds us, "He who walks with wise men will be wise, But the companion of fools will suffer harm." We keep listening to Scripture about these negative voices in Ephesians 5:6–7, "See that no one deceives you with empty words, for because of these things the wrath of God comes upon the sons of disobedience. Therefore do not become partners with them."

There are some people in our lives who have caused us great dismay. One person I know hoped all her life that her father would ask forgiveness for his ill treatment of her before he died. Well, it didn't happen. When other people make choices to treat us unfairly, and the resolve we wish for doesn't happen, we must not hold ourselves hostage for their bad behavior.

Negative voices keeping us depressed cripple our positive development. That hostage factor is too real. Others who have a problem need to answer for their stuff and we must give up being understood. It might not happen. They might never be capable, and we need to proceed free in Jesus as much as their behaviors are not right. It's Jesus who draws the lines; we don't have to. We place our faith in God, not people or we'll often be disappointed (and unhappy). He hears when I cry and others may not. We're all broken, but God sorts it all out.

Our outlook goes back to our foundation, our core, whether we're a secure or troubled person. When our house is built on the sand and the rain comes down, we can wash away. As we go further in this book, seeing how God fits in to avoid this destructive state of insecurity, we'll be motivated to run away from negative voices producing negative consequences. Let's not be one of those lifers who insist on the theme of "the other person wrecked my life, I'll never make it; I can't do it; there's no way because I'm not good enough!" If that's your decision, you will fail. You get to choose your own prophecy and consequence.

The book of Proverbs is full of descriptions of a fool. Those folks are obviously not living after the heart of God. Life's immediate impulses end up taking priority over the truth. The more familiar we become with a fool's description the more we can be motivated to refuse to go that route ourselves. Proverbs 12:15 says, "The way of a fool is right in his own eyes." One reason is we let blind spots develop because we don't have a clue how this negative progression of voices takes place and pulls us down. The calendar of blank spots we have already observed gives us an idea of why we are missing key pieces to avoid a downward spiral. Another factor is the fool who knows the right thing and just keeps their fist in God's face with the attitude that they deserve whatever they want and now. They feel so victimized. We'll look at these people later in the book.

We've also observed the arrow of the gravity flow downward in a previous chapter, showing what it's like with the old nature in our lives. We've observed it in our life and especially observed it in others, right? The natural way just happens until we turn the wheel and go a different

The Downward Spiral

BLANK SPOTS
ARE
BLIND SPOTS
BECAUSE
UNFAMILIARITY
BREEDS
INDIFFERENCE
BREEDS
DECEPTION
BREEDS
LOSS OF
PERSPECTIVE

IMMEDIATE IMPULSES
TAKE PRIORITY
OVER THE TRUTH

direction. The more those **blank spots** are present the more **blind spots** we possess. We just go with the flow around us—*ho hum, consequences don't matter as I'm having fun doing what I want.* Things don't matter if we follow the life track around us that is contrary to the written design of our almighty God. Our minds are clouded and it's a slippery slope. We don't realize we're like the frog in the beaker, boiling to death a degree at a time.

You may not realize it yet, but the Bible does tell us the devil "prowls around like a roaring lion, seeking someone to devour" (1 Pet. 5:8). Very smart people are being deceived while becoming victims unaware of the trickery. Information withheld or rear-ranged to look like the truth skillfully blinds their eyes. Half-truths can sound so good, but the incomplete nature of it all causes this misinformation to guide our mind's choices in the wrong direction.

Are we boiling to death a degree at a time?

Withholding facts causes falsehood to reign. So then, these smart people will end up saying, "I just didn't realize . . ." Are you boiling to death a degree at a time, and not having a clue? People around us are saying one thing but meaning another. It's a big deal that we understand the evil nature of this falsehood trend.

Avoiding knowing God and His will in the Scriptures sets us up for negative voices. We're just flat-out unfamiliar with what God has said, and furthermore, we don't really care. When we're **unfamiliar**, it breeds **forgetfulness**. The Bible calls that being "dull of hearing" (Heb. 5:11 NASB95), and then goes on to say, "For though by this time you ought to be teachers, you have need again for someone to teach you the elementary principles of the actual words of God." The principles are not obvious enough anymore and we are off about our merry way.

Verse 14 then says its "because of practice [they] have their senses trained to distinguish between good and evil." Unfamiliarity is because of not training those senses to discern so we forget whatever we might have known. (That word *practice* in the Greek is where we get our word *gymnasium*, where we go to work out our bodies for skill, proficiency, and endurance.) What a great picture for us to work out our minds in the Word. We need it to offset all negativity.

The forgetfulness breeds **indifference**. We compare ourselves to others and say, "I'm not so bad." We become hardened to the truth. We act as if we are our God and whatever we say or want needs to happen. We play with fire and set ourselves to get burned. Not nice.

That indifference breeds **deception**. I'm just standing against the wrong ruler or standard. Pleasure overrides the truth. The term *fool* applies to such a person. They believe half-truths and can rationalize anything or argue that they are okay. You've heard yourself or others give many reasons of why they are right. They might say, I need, I want, or I deserve whatever because I have it coming. Such deception. They work so hard to prove they are right.

Do I know God's principles for me?

Deception breeds **a loss of perspective**; they'll find themselves avoiding those people who want to make a big deal out of their bad choices. They get overindulged and put God to the test. Too many will claim God has let them down as they are suppressing the truth. **The immediate impulses then take priority over the truth.** Living on the edge is so destructive. Family members are left in disbelief and the cause of Christ is severely damaged. The godly standard has been violated, as has the standard setter.

This downward spiral shows itself in numbers of ways. We'd best be aware of dark forces in our world, so we studiously take specific steps to avoid being swept away. The pulls are strong. You need protective habits if you will, to stay away. The dark forces destroy you, your loved ones, and others who are close. Trying their "rabbit holes" can lead you into an abyss that reforms your mind the wrong way. It can convince you that wrong is right and that things you once knew as right are no longer good for you.

It's interesting how people who don't feel secure or safe feel compelled to latch on to something to feel powerful. Wrong friends, uncensored internet, shady movies, and so much more can be influential here. Maybe it's wrong treatment that has driven them to something that seems so good. I don't even want to start naming the many totally destructive, dark practices people start indulging.

The apostle Paul in Romans 7:15–17 expresses how he got caught up in knowing better but doing wrong. "For I do not understand what I am doing; for I am not practicing what I want to do, but I am doing the very thing I hate. However, if I do the very thing I do not want to do, I agree with the Law, that the Law is good. But now, no longer am I the one doing it, but sin that dwells in me."

There are too many Satanic forces in the world providing false security. Outwardly they can sound like there's hope and power if you indulge in their beliefs and practices. Lies are everywhere. If you do a word study on deception and falsehood, you'll be overwhelmed at the powers of evil around us swaying even smart people into believing pure falsehood. The consequences are ugly.

Unexpected, bizarre behaviors surface in people we thought were solid in their Christian faith, people who appeared to have a godly life on the outside. Ephesians 6:11–12 reminds us we need to "be able to stand firm against the schemes of the devil. For our struggle is not against flesh and blood, but against the rulers, against the powers, against the world forces of this darkness, against the spiritual forces of wickedness in the heavenly places."

The need to belong is strong—let's beware of what we are attaching ourselves to. Needs that we want satisfied must have a *pattern from above*. Our lens must not be clouded so as not to see the wrong goal out there. It's just too natural to start talking like those around us. "I deserve." "I'll do as I please." "I have a right to what I want." "I'll make you pay." "Nothing matters anymore." "I'm better than you."

We're not going to delve into the depths of naming or describing the practices of devilish organizations, but a word to the wise is sufficient. **Be careful and aware.** They are real and powerful and ready to take you down.

Your needs for power and acceptance and hope must come from the only true Source—a growing, committed relationship to the living God. Chapter 9 on the God-factor will give you tracks to run on.

I'll lend a few observations of evil forces from my experience. In a high school PE class during what must have been some down time, I observed some unusual powers. I saw four girls lift a Ouija board off a table without touching it. Spooky. I stayed away.

Then, a young person in our community was playing around with a Ouija board. She had messages that she would likely die. Sure enough, a freak accident took her life not long after.

One day a usually okay worker came to my house. She happened to tell me she had been out in the woods with some guys doing strange things. I could see her eyes were not normal and her behavior was very unusual. I'd never been around a demon-possessed person but this seemed like a first. I encouraged her to leave, and I proceeded to go through the rooms and exorcize them, praying to remove the obvious evil influences she brought with her. Her demons appeared very real.

You don't have to be demon-possessed to have negative voices, but the evil one definitely desires us to live after his designs, and they are negative. Unfortunately, human nature often does not allow us to see ourselves as we really are. It would be smart if we would get honest with ourselves and ask if the following ungodly characteristics are us or not. What do people keep seeing in us? How are we affecting people around us? What is causing people around me to be hurt by my actions? Am I being honest to evaluate myself for my sake and everybody around me? Let's see here how we might make some adjustments for everybody's good. I encourage you to spend some time thinking about each of these very common maladies below and ask yourself if this is really you.

When we lose true perspective, we become deceived with many negative ways of life, and these undesirable qualities take over:

- a self-orientation, as it's all about me
- entitlement
- hypocrisy
- disobedience
- refusal to let go so always in angst
- expect darkness so I fulfill that

- disrespect
- arrogance
- hurt others to feel better about one's self
- structure failure into each day
- pursue ruin, as that is my life of familiarity
- disobedience to laws
- untruthfulness
- immoral
- dishonesty/cheating

- unrealistic
- need to retaliate to feel good about self
- elongates pain and problems
- stressed over everything
- sees self as superior
- unhappy
- complaining
- not flexible
- not rational
- not seeing others
- bondage is preferred

- my assessments are out of proportion
- demand my control and change
- tantrums abound
- mind blown over small things
- need to dwell on others' failures

- always overwhelmed, so can't be productive
- panic oriented
- perfection expected
- jealous and covetous

- pout to get my way
- unaccepting of loss

- unforgiving
- self-justification
- unable to cope with anything
- unequally yoked in marriage or business
- cannot cope
- blame and shame

- self-deluded
- bitter
- frantic
- nothing is enough
- refuse reality
- out of control
- in despair
- broken

Psalm 1:1–2 says, "Blessed is the person who does not walk in the counsel of the wicked, Nor stand in the path of sinners, Nor sit in the seat of scoffers! But his delight is in the Law of the Lord, And on His

Law he meditates day and night." The reminders are here—don't let the negative voices in our culture influence your life (walking next to, standing with, or sitting down with). There are consequences.

Negative voices come from men and women who prefer the darkness. John 3:19–20 speaks this clearly, "people loved the darkness rather than the Light, for their deeds were evil. For everyone who does evil hates the Light, and does not come to the Light, so that his deeds will be exposed." It's hard to watch such people who simply cannot see themselves. They can, however, find fault with everybody else.

It's important we understand this force so we are not taken down with it. Philippians 3:18–19 spells out more of the same, "many . . . are the enemies of the cross of Christ, whose end is destruction, whose god is their appetite, and whose glory is in their shame, who have their minds on earthly things."

In what groups do you place yourself and the kinds of conversations you listen to? They become powers of suggestions for you. Is failure an ongoing theme among your groups? It is okay to fail as we all do at times but to focus on it instead of looking for the good will not benefit anybody. People like Abraham Lincoln failed thirty-two times in his personal, business, and political pursuits, but that didn't keep him down. Circles you frequent need to have a true view of God, from the Scriptures, thus it is of upmost importance you are acutely aware of negative voices that would lead you in the wrong direction.

How do you fact-check anything? Does anyone have the right to change definitions, of even gender God created? Just because somebody calls something "misinformation" doesn't mean it is. You need to know from your own sources of knowledge what is right. Let's look at our Bibles and see what the definitions of anything are. Back to renaming things, mothers being referred to as a birthing person now is not smart. No, there is a lot to being a mother by God's expectations, not just going through the physical birth process. Sympathies to the child who doesn't have a mom to help develop their life, through birth or being adopted.

Sometimes, it's the-sky-is-falling attitude, or many illustrations of victimhood that come up frequently. We'll get to that subject in more detail in chapter 14 (Understanding victimhood, narcissism and entitlement.). The bottom line of all the negative talk stems from the schemes of the devil. "For our struggle is not against flesh and blood, but against the rulers, against the powers, against the world forces of this darkness, against the spiritual forces of wickedness in the heavenly places" (Eph. 6:12).

It goes on in verse 16, "in addition to all, taking up the shield of faith with which you will be able to extinguish all the flaming arrows of the evil one." There's trouble out there on all sides of us and we need to be prepared to deal with these negative voices and negative forces to not be taken down. They'll take you out where you are weakest.

You definitely need to keep your guard up so the negative mindset does not describe you. In the book of 2 Timothy (chapter 3 is full of it) he describes it this way:

Difficult times	Love only self and money
Boastful	Proud
Scoffing at God	Disobedient to parents
Nothing sacred	Unloving
Unforgiving	Slander
No self-control	Cruel
Hate good	Betray friends
Reckless	Puffed up/prideful
Love pleasure, rather than God	Reject power

With a society shouting that these anti-God qualities are normal, we'd best get our prevention system going strong. This culture has watered down the standard. Jeremiah 17:5, 9 says, "Cursed is the man who trusts in mankind And makes flesh his strength, And whose heart turns away from the Lord. . . .The heart is more deceitful than all else And is desperately sick; Who can understand it?"

Thomas Sowell said, "We seem to be getting closer and closer to a situation where nobody is responsible for what they did but we are all responsible for what somebody else did."[2] Oh that we would take responsibility for our own personal issues of allowing negative responses to prevail and not blame others.

So what are some more common negative voices you face? Maybe you'll identify with some of these, and then make sure you shore up your defenses to not let them take you under.

- It'll never work
- You always do it wrong
- You can't overcome this
- You're not allowed to proceed
- You always give me the short end of the deal
- It's all your fault
- You complain about everything
- You're never meeting my needs
- You don't need . . .
- You don't help me
- You are the problem
- You don't know enough

- What makes you think you are right?
- You take after your relatives
- What you believe is all wrong
- You had this coming

- You never take responsibility
- You embarrass me

- You shouldn't try
- When are you going to learn?
- Your background disables you
- I know you won't listen
- I'm better than you are at . . .

- You're a liar
- Why would you do this?
- You're always distracted
- You're not good at . . .
- You're too old and out of shape
- You might as well quit
- You have no clue what you are doing

- You'll just mess up my plan

- You're in my way
- You don't deserve . . .
- You are too untrustworthy to proceed

- You don't work hard enough

So, what's our response to negative voices and troubles? What did Jesus do when He did not like bad behaviors? Ephesians 4:26–27, "BE ANGRY AND YET DO NOT SIN. . . . Do not give the devil an opportunity." Jesus also turned over tables of sinners in the temple when they were wrong.

We definitely don't like injustice and get angry, but our response is key. Our learning how to respond to people needs to be like artwork with word choices. You think very carefully through it all, don't ignore it, but use **careful words** that wouldn't violate God's instructions. It **takes work** to do it right. And a bad life pattern of response will sting you.

Is our reasoning on the surface or can it go deeper to discover root causes of our life responses? It'll save you many frustrations and years of counseling dollars as you look at God's intentions and choose to match up. It's the life instruction book that will guide you with insights beyond the natural way to activate powers of positivity.

The following list of frequent poor responses to negative voices happen because of personal issues, like fear, jealousy, anger, childhood habits, insecurity, falsehood, a false trust, skewed thinking, and more.

What would be some poor responses to negative voices:

• Retribution, make life miserable for the other

• Pass on your anger to everybody you know

• Sit around whining

• Ignore truth

• Self-protect

• Harbor your bad feelings forever

• Make unreasonable demands

• Throw fits, act like a child

• Try to prove your worth to feel better

• Return the "favor"

• "I have a right to be angry and get even"

• Throw away precious relationships

• Live chaotically with everything

• Abandon your spouse, kids, friends, church

• Shun others who have been close

• Start some addiction

• Plead that it is your parents' fault

• Run away hard in the wrong direction

• Choose to magnify the hardship

• Excuse everything

• Transfer the blame

• Bury yourself in excessive spending or running away

• Expect others to soothe your inward pain

• Insist that God let you down

• Raise a fist in God's face

• Refuse to be happy or let go of whatever

- Undermine others

- Give no credence to the other side of the story

- Refuse help

- Sometimes suicide

- Continue to rehearse the dark side of your perception

- Take somebody down

- Tell lies about other people, set them up to fail

When we handle situations poorly, we can expect tough consequences. People oft become hopeless, as it sucks the air out of everybody involved. Depression sets in with a desire to retreat.

Scripture speaks truth to us: "Everyone who hears these words of Mine and does not act on them, will be like a foolish man who built his house on the sand. And the rain fell and the floods came, and the winds blew and slammed against that house; and it fell—and its collapse was great" (Matt. 7:26–27). When there are negative voices in our lives, we'd best not build our house on the sand, because there will be destruction.

Where do your thoughts go when imperfection surfaces, like when you didn't make the cut somewhere or when you were persecuted? The levels of intensity range all over the map but the bottom-line question remains. Is my foundation solid and do I believe it will help me handle the toughest life assignments? Remember, diamonds are made under pressure.

Some people grew up soft and never had to go through much adversity. They had loving parents, money to meet all their needs, and no significant losses. Everything happened to go quite well for these few. They had everything given to them and did not experience a lot of negative voices and trends. These people will find it harder as adults to figure out a new way to respond when things start going badly, when they didn't expect it. They can learn though.

Another aspect of negative people is described in mental health circles as *psychological projection*. Brad Lyles, MD, describes it this way: "Psychological projection hardens a patient's mere belief or suspicion that the *other* (person, organization) is bad into a *conviction* the other person is bad. In particular, the patient *knows* the other person is bad." Further, he talks about how people are "accusing the other guy of what [they] are doing."[3] Be aware these people exist around us. We need to choose to only listen to people who are on the right track in life. No derailments allowed.

We can look at the negatives we face as hurdlers do with their race. Successful people will realize they learn to jump those hurdles to win their races. So when we think the grass is greener on the other side of the fence, as a successful person, we learn to jump those hurdles. We'll cover more how-tos as we go along here. But for a few tips now, "You won't get out of a mess by making another one" and "Feed your fears and your faith will starve."[4]

Everything will help when we see ourselves accurately, when we get next to the right people who can influence us positively, and point us in the best direction. Thus, that means we need to run hard from the negative voices near and far. What and who are your influences? This does matter, just as your mindset matters.

Study Questions for Chapter 5: Negative Voices and Trends

1. Study the deceiving voice Eve heard in the garden as her eyes were tempted. See Genesis 3:6.

2. Give several illustrations of how we can be tempted when we see something and know it's been forbidden.

3. Read aloud some Scriptures of the behavior of fools. Do a word study and share your findings.

4. Regarding Ephesians 5:6–7, discuss what empty words are and what do they lead to? Give some illustrations from your life observations. What is the wrath of God going to look like? What is the warning we best heed?

5. When people in our lives continue to cause us dismay with negative attitudes, words, and actions, can we count on them changing? Discuss forgiveness and share Scriptures we need to adhere to. Who

is the loser when we don't forgive? See the quote on psychological projection at the end of the chapter. How best do we deal with negative people?

6. Explain the reality of the old nature we're born with and how the progression of sin escalates as shown in "the downward spiral" seen in this chapter. Read the chart aloud and give some illustrations of real-life observations you've made.

7. Why and how do we get into the position of being like the frog boiling to death? Discuss the Hebrews 5:11–14 passage.

8. Did Paul succumb to following negative voices? See Romans 7:15–17.

9. How does the Bible describe negative forces? See Ephesians 6:11–12.

10. Review the negative qualities you want to be certain to refuse in your life. Read many of them, as seen in the chapter, so you're extra aware to disallow them.

11. Notice the verbs in Psalm 1:1–2 and how they reflect three levels of participation in the counsel of the wicked.

12. Why do we do evil? See John 3:19–20 and Philippians 3:18–19.

13. Why are there negative voices around us? See Jeremiah 17:5, 9.

14. List some negative voices we hear and begin to believe.

15. What does Scripture say we should do with negative voices? See Ephesians 4:26–27.

16. What is the result of our choosing foolish responses? See Matthew 7:26–27.

6

Setbacks and Trials

We all have setbacks of one kind and another. It feels like nobody could have a clue about the things WE are going through. Our life tapestry is so full of knots it seems nobody observing could see any worthwhileness. So we can relate to how this person feels in the graphic—hopeless and defeated. Life is not easy. C. S. Lewis says, "God whispers to us in our pleasures, speaks in our conscience, but shouts in our pains: it is his megaphone to rouse a deaf world."[1]

Because so much bombards us, we must decide beforehand what our general mindset is going to be so we can handle it all with grace and not panic or fall apart. Many things take us totally by surprise, so we'd best put on our spiritual armor for the fight ahead. Ephesians 6:11, 13 says, "Put on the full armor of God, so that you will be able to stand firm against the schemes of the devil. . . . that you may be able to resist on the evil day, and having done everything, to stand firm."

Feeling hopeless?

Being prepared when those surprises happen is so essential. When my sister Judy and her husband, Rick, lost their firstborn son to a horrific accidental drowning, none of us felt at all prepared. Such pain and grief sent us to rely on our big God for strength to continue. This was a huge setback and trial through which to demonstrate our faith.

Part of our country experiences large fires and hurricanes and floods forcing families to leave everything they own and move to safer areas to save their lives. A couple years ago for the first time I needed to pack our two vehicles with everything I considered valuable because we were at level 2 evacuation. (A week later I unpacked and all was fine.) It's not easy leaving your earthly treasures. Worse yet is a violent area where people's lives are at risk and others are dying so horribly. Then there are the surprises of massive strokes, heart attacks, and accidents that injure our loved ones or take their lives forever. So devastating. Maybe it's a mental health or dementia crisis in your family disrupting everything. The loss of income from jobs disappearing is more than disheartening. Look at this list of crises and hardships. Would you be described as complacent or hopeless as the enemy strikes where you're the weakest?

Injustices, cheating, robbery
Violations, sinned against, persecutions

Inequities, rejection, dishonesty
Losses of family members to death or abandonment, of jobs, of health

Injuries
Destruction of our relationships, our homes, our businesses

Tragedies
Failures to produce

Discouragements, disappointments

Abuse (physically, psychologically)

Brick walls, misrepresentation
Burdens to bear, disrespect paid
Disallowed to be who you are
Mockery, overpowering

Barbed wire entrances, disallowed
Manipulation and control
False witness against you

The chips are down, you'll say. *I got a bad deal. I got hurt or diseased. The odds are against me and I'll never get through this. Life is hard. Relationships are too sour. People hurt me. Circumstances go south. I couldn't make the team or get into the college I wanted.*

It's healthy to observe people who have gone before us and learn by observing their determination. As we noted before, Abraham Lincoln lost elections, lost close family to death, and had huge disappointments at least thirty-two times before he was elected the president of the United States. Job in the Scriptures lost everything he owned and suffered from terrible sickness. Both of these men still confessed their trust in Almighty God through it all. God restored both these men and their lives from huge devastation to greater things on the other side.

So what is my strategy in playing out this hand? I know people who have been wrongfully sued, people who have been treated oh so unfairly. The hard thing is to keep on moving in the right direction they know to be true. We need to find our "big person" response instead of going under. And to do that skillfully we'd best realize it's the Lord God who will give us the wisdom and guidance we need. He will enable us to change "stinkin' thinkin'" to a recycled way to approach our woes.

Fortunately, "Storms never last. The night always gives way to the Sonrise. One season always yields to the next. So, too, our human impossibilities become divine miracles. We need only trust and wait."[2] When we ride in an airplane and lift off toward the clouds, it is such a pleasure when we break through it all and experience the blue skies. Such pleasure to rise above.

By using each of our trials as learning experiences to be better people on the other side, we transform them as stepping stones for good things ahead. I'm sure you have many examples of situations that are wrong, unfair, and devastating. We have had family members wrongfully not allowed to cross a border. Many friends are going through very deep waters physically; does that seem fair? We have numerous friends who have broken their marriage covenants. We all have long stories.

What does the Bible say about the good that can come from these many trials? It's helpful to have a word from our ultimate plumb line when we feel all the pressures mounting on us and we need to know why it's happening. Second Corinthians 1:8–10 talks about being "burdened excessively, beyond our strength, so that we despaired even of life. Indeed, we had the sentence of death within ourselves." Then, it gives us the reason for this: "so that we **would not trust in ourselves, but in God** who raises the dead; who rescued us from so great a danger of death, and will rescue us, He on whom we have set our hope. And

He will yet deliver us." It's too easy to try and trust in ourselves to get through the hard things.

There are answers for *why* we have trials, there are *promises to claim* during these trials, and there are *personal responsibilities* we must meet during these trials. Looking at all three aspects here, let's consider 1 Peter 5:6–10:

> Humble yourselves under the mighty hand of God, so that He may exalt you at the proper time, having casting all your anxiety on Him, because He cares about you. Be of sober spirit, be on the alert. Your adversary, the devil prowls around like a roaring lion, seeking someone to devour. But resist him, firm in your faith, knowing that the same experiences of suffering are being accomplished by your brothers and sisters who are in the world. After you have suffered for a little while, the God of all grace, who called you to His eternal glory in Christ, will Himself perfect, confirm, strengthen, and establish you.

Are you spotting all three pieces to the trials we face? The repetition of it all helps these concepts sink in—the mother of all learning, they say.

Another passage in Scripture demonstrates these three aspects of the trials Joshua encountered. I'll hope you go for "extra credit" and look up Joshua 1:5–9 and see God's healing power for brokenness demonstrated.

There are lesser situations to deal with causing us angst as well. Some years back I worked as a travel agent for a season. With my occasional free ticket option, I arranged a trip to meet a friend at her business location. This "trial" doesn't come anywhere close to other people's large challenges. I hadn't realized my plane was making a stop in route to my destination. Then, in front of the entire plane, the flight attendant asked if I was Linda Weber. "I'm going to have to ask you to deplane." *You're kidding*, I thought. I was flying on a low priority ticket so I had to get off and figure out what to do next. This was before cell phones so I had no way to contact my friend to tell her why I wasn't arriving as planned. Furthermore, I didn't even know what hotel we were going to since she made the plans and would have been taking me there. It was a stressful time but not like so many other things we experience.

Another airplane experience gave me an opportunity to face possible death. This trial was more severe, obviously. The pilot told us our flaps were not descending and we were going to fly for a while to deplete our fuel supply. He told us a speedy landing could cause the tires to burst and there was danger of fire and explosion. I asked the man sitting by me if he was ready to meet his Maker. He said no, so we got into a discussion about how to face eternity. The runway was lined with many emergency vehicles for our possible demise. I write this years later telling you that all went well but it was an opportunity to choose to respond in a positive manner. This gentleman even expressed how he detected I was a confident person. This high-level government man even called me a year later to tell me how he came to resolve some trials he had.

What are some words spoken about trials? First Corinthians 10:11–13 says, "Now these things happened to them as an example, and they were written for our instruction. . . . Therefore let the one who thinks he stands watch out that he does not fall. . . . God is faithful, so He will not allow you to be tempted beyond what you are able, but with the temptation will provide the way of escape also, so that you will be able to endure it." Do we *want* to hear it's for our instruction? No, but we're also told God will provide a way of escape. *Thank You, Lord. I needed that.* He draws us to Himself through pain and hard experiences. He offers us hope.

As the ancient proverb says, "If we dwell [on our trials] on the past, we lose an eye. If we forget the past, we lose both eyes." There are purposes to learn from history.

We can be our own worst enemy, having come from prior bad patterns of living, which has been what's familiar. And, then we reproduce what has been familiar, making us the producer of more bad experiences because that's what we know how to do. We are the ones creating our own new hardships, and don't even realize it. Unknowingly, we think we're making ourselves comfortable with the familiar, as crazy as that sounds. These situations are all too common, and it's usually the case that the person with this large problem cannot see themselves doing *it to themselves*. They've got it all figured out how it's the other guy's fault and they proceed to blame, shame, and create division. They might give you fifty reasons how they are right. They really think this trial is the other guy's problem and not theirs. And they can skillfully argue it all day long.

Then, there are plenty of times the problems we face are not instigated by us. I'll share what my friend, Elliette Harrison, wrote those in her sphere who were experiencing issues:

> Praying that whatever battle you find yourself in today . . . you will have eyes to see and ears to hear. Asking God to be the rock under your feet when the whole world feels like it is shaking. Our Father is intimate with us and sees our struggle, fear and doubt. Hold tight to the promises He has given us…promises to prosper and not harm us. Plans to give us HOPE and a future. Do not get weighed down by the lies of the enemy who tells you "this situation is hopeless." Our Father shines in the face of the impossible and He will walk with you through every struggle. In our weakness, His power is made perfect and His grace IS sufficient. Trust Him. Trust Him. Trust Him.

Then she quotes Ephesians 6:12–13: "Our struggle is not against flesh and blood, but against the rulers, against the powers, against the world-forces of this darkness, against the spiritual forces of wickedness in the heavenly places. Therefore, take up the full armor of God that you may be able to resist in the evil day, and having done everything, to stand firm."[3] We just heard that, didn't we?

Often with trials we find ourselves fearful of the unknowns. We don't know how or what or why and in our insecurity we don't feel SAFE. Our culture has taught this response, to fear whatever. Besides the culture, we often **get trained and prepared to fear** within our family of origin systems. It will be smart of us to identify this reality and take on different God-designed patterns. Psalm 56:2–4 says, "My enemies have trampled upon me all day long, For they are many who fight proudly against me. When I am afraid, I will put my trust in You. In God, whose word I praise, In God I have put my trust; I *shall not be* *afraid.*" We don't want to be guilty of running or hiding or refusing the blessing of God's safety.

Things happen and our feelings come into play. If you were a tree, you'd feel like that description in Psalm 1:3, "withering." Your productivity is zapped from all the disasters you face. You might feel you just cannot deal with another issue. You have many examples popping into your head about what you have faced in life that makes you feel like the withering tree.

Withering from trials

My heart goes out to spouses whose mates have passed away from one thing and another and you are left with many pieces in life to face. Then, of course, many marriages break up because one partner abandons the other, for selfish reasons, leaving the spouse in a most withering state of mind. It's devastating to have these families break up. Those who have lost their "kids" in war, in unfortunate accidents, disease, or maybe it's the kids deciding they have no desire to honor their parents anymore and even abandon the relationship. So much devastation. All of this simply brings us to our knees in disbelief. For you, maybe it's losing a parent whether in old age or when they were quite young—it is all so hard.

There are all kinds of losses besides deaths—health or the ability to function normally, jobs with income, promotions deserved but not given, a pet's death, fire taking a home or business, etc.

Maybe it's like an earthquake has hit and you've fallen through the cracks with nobody to help you out. You might have had a dysfunctional home with one or both parents who gave you no good examples. Your siblings act like you don't exist. Your spouse treats you with disrespect. There is no money to work with and no jobs to help you out. There are too many things wrong with your house you're unable to get repaired, or your neighbors have been noisy and invasive to your property. Maybe at school you were discriminated against and given unfair grades and the athletic program felt you weren't good enough. Your health has deteriorated badly and you can't function very well. Your friends basically traded you for others they liked better. Perhaps you even got sued by some money-thirsty acquaintance who totally violated the truth. To make matters worse, you lost what money you invested in a sure deal and were left with basically nothing.

Let's just say things in life are not always going as we hope. I've personally always felt if plan A doesn't work, I go to plan B, and then plan C. If I get to the end of the alphabet, I need to start over at AA, then to BB, and CC. It's okay. Resolve for things doesn't just happen; it takes ongoing work and determination to work with alternatives.

Some disappointments are not as life changing as others on the scale of things, but they present challenges we did not anticipate. When we were away from home for a few days, I felt at such a loss when I got a call from the police that our storage unit was broken into. It was so disappointing to have possessions violated. We got a few things back but not all. Sometimes bad things just happen.

Another of my disappointments—though not severe—related to academics. I had a 3.84 grade average in high school, all the activities, good references, and a strong desire to continue to do well in school. My future husband was at Wheaton College in Illinois, and I wanted to go there too. My SATs weren't high and that kept me from being admitted. In hindsight, I now see I would have been there for only a year or two before my new husband and I would have been off to four years in the Army and four years of seminary. I would have had to go in debt to cover what wasn't by scholarships and that would have set us back quite far. So it was best, and yet I wasn't thinking that way at the time.

It's quite obvious life is not perfect, to say the least. Did the characters in the Bible ever experience trouble to the point they were unusable by God? Hardly. Were there hardships—yes, for sure. Abraham was quite old but look how God used him. Jacob was a liar. Moses had a stuttering problem. Joseph was abused. Isaac was a daydreamer. Sampson was a womanizer. David really did blow it—had a man killed so he could take his wife. Martha worried about everything. Zaccheus was small, but that didn't stop his influence. Gideon made excuses from his fears. Elijah was suicidal, Job went bankrupt. Rahab was a prostitute.

Peter even denied Christ. Did you notice the disciples fell asleep while praying and had very little faith? God used these people, and He can use us too. Never forget how our God is a God of redemption through it all.

Dwelling on the myriad troubles we face only extends our pain. In the middle of all the traumas, we must get our heads turned around so we see God. He will be to us everything we need whether in times of plenty or in want.

Micah 7:8 says, "Though I fall I will rise; though I live in darkness, the LORD is a light for me." He is that light we need; He is our Redeemer, our Savior, our guide, our peace, our joy, and our comfort. We are humbled He wants a relationship with us. He will never leave us, never forsake us, never mislead us, never forget us, and never overlook us!

> When we fall—You lift us!
> When we fail—You forgive!
> When we are weak—You are our strength!
> When we are lost—You are the way!
> When we are afraid—You are our courage!
> When we stumble—You steady us!
> When we are hurt—You heal us!
> When we are broken—You mend us!
> When we are blind—You lead us!
> When we are hungry—You feed us!
> When we face trials—You are with us!
> When we face persecution—You shield us!
> When we face loss—You provide for us!
> When we face death—You carry us home!"[4]

We don't exactly like to hear He has a plan for trials to make us better people. When we can't understand what's going on in life, we must go back to the basics. Let's spend some time here and observe what God says in His Word about trials. We can develop resilience when we discern from Scripture how God would have us think about our trials and how to respond His way.

- "And we know that God causes all things to work together for good to those who love God, to those who are called according to His purpose. . . . If God is for us, who is against us? . . . Who shall separate us from the love of Christ? Will tribulation, or trouble, or persecution, or famine, or nakedness, or peril, or sword? . . . But in all these things we

Our mental file drawers

overwhelmingly conquer through Him who loved us. For I am convinced that neither death, nor life, nor angels, nor principalities, nor things present, nor things to come, nor powers, nor height, nor depth, nor any other created thing will be able to separate us from the love of God that is in Christ Jesus our Lord" (Rom 8:28, 31, 35, 37–39). That ought to do it for us. We're covered, through everything we endure. We're good.

- [Because of our position in Christ] ". . . we also celebrate in our tribulations, knowing that tribulation brings about perseverance; and perseverance, proven character; and proven character, hope; and hope does not disappoint because the love of God has been poured out within our hearts through the Holy Spirit who was given to us" (Rom. 5:3–5).
- "For our momentary, light affliction is producing for us an eternal weight of glory far beyond all comparison, while we look not at the things which are seen, but at the things which are not seen; for the things which are seen are temporal, but the things which are not seen are eternal" (2 Cor. 4:17–18).
- "After you have suffered for a little while, the God of all grace, who called you to His eternal glory in Christ, will Himself perfect, confirm, strengthen, and establish you" (1 Pet. 5:10).
- "When all kinds of trials and temptations crowd into your lives, my brothers, don't resent them as intruders, but welcome them as friends! Realize that they come to test your faith and to produce in you the quality of endurance. But let the process go on until that endurance is fully developed, and you will find

you have become men of mature character with the right sort of independence. And if, in the process, any of you does not know how to meet any particular problem he has only to ask God—who gives generously to all men without making them feel foolish or guilty—and he may be quite sure that the necessary wisdom will be given him" (Phillips). (I enjoyed memorizing this years ago for my forever recall.) James 1:2-5

- "Blessed is a man who perseveres under trial; for once he has been approved, he will receive the crown of life which the Lord has promised to those who love Him. No one is to say when he is tempted, 'I am being tempted by God'; for God cannot be tempted by evil, and He Himself does not tempt anyone" (James 1:12–13).

- "From the end of the earth I call to You when my heart is faint; Lead me to the rock that is higher than I. For You have been a refuge for me, A tower of strength against the enemy. Let me dwell in Your tent forever; Let me take refuge in the shelter of Your wings" (Ps. 61:2–4).

- "Do not be surprised at the fiery ordeal among you, which comes upon you for your testing, as though some strange thing were happening to you; but to the degree that you share the sufferings of Christ, keep on rejoicing, so that also at the revelation of His glory you may also rejoice and be overjoyed. . . . Therefore, those also who suffer according to the will of God are to entrust their souls to a faithful Creator in doing what is right" (1 Pet. 4:12–13, 19).

- "Not that I speak from need, for I have learned to be content in whatever circumstances I am. I know how to get along with little, and I also know how to live in prosperity; in any and every circumstance I have learned the secret of being filled and going hungry, both of having abundance and suffering need. I can do all things through Him who strengthens me" (Phil. 4:11–13).

- ". . . we do not lose heart. . . . 'light shall shine out of darkness'. . . . the extraordinary greatness of the power will be of God and not from ourselves; we are afflicted in every way, but not crushed; perplexed, but not despairing; persecuted, but not abandoned;

struck down, but not destroyed . . . so that the life of Jesus also may be manifested in our body. . . . For our momentary, light affliction is producing for us an eternal weight of glory far beyond all comparison, while we look not at the things which are seen, but at the things which are not seen; for the things which are seen are temporal, but the things which are not seen are eternal" (2 Cor. 3:1, 6–10, 17–18).

- "God is our refuge and strength, A very ready help in trouble. Therefore we will not fear, though the earth shakes And the mountains slip into the heart of the sea; Though its waters roar and foam, Though the mountains quake at its swelling pride. . . . The LORD of armies is with us; The God of Jacob is our stronghold" (Ps. 46:1–3, 7).

- "The LORD also will be a stronghold for the oppressed, A stronghold in times of trouble; And those who know Your name will put their trust in You, For You, LORD, have not abandoned those who seek You" (Ps. 9:9–10).

- "Even though I walk through the valley of the shadow of death, I fear no evil, for You are with me; Your rod and Your staff, they comfort me. You prepare a table before me in the presence of my enemies; You have anointed my head with oil; My cup overflows. Certainly goodness and faithfulness will follow me all the days of my life, And my dwelling will be in the house of the LORD forever" (Ps. 23:4–7).

- "When evildoers came upon me to devour my flesh, My adversaries and my enemies, they stumbled and fell. . . . My heart will not fear; If war arise against me, In spite of this I am confident. . . . For on the day of trouble He will conceal me in His tabernacle; He will hide me in the secret place of His tent; He will lift me up on a rock. And now my head will be lifted up above my enemies around me" (Ps. 27:2–3, 5–6).

- ". . . in Me you may have peace. In the world you have tribulation, but take courage; I have overcome the world" (John 16:33).

- "For I consider that the sufferings of this present time are not worthy to be compared with the glory that is to be revealed to us. . . . If we hope for what we do not see, through perseverance we wait eagerly for it" (Rom. 8:18, 25).

- ". . . if necessary, you have been distressed by various trials, so that the proof of your faith, being more precious than gold which perishes though tested by fire, may be found to result in praise, glory, and honor at the revelation of Jesus Christ" (1 Pet. 1:6–7).

- "Blessed are those who have been persecuted for the sake of righteousness, for theirs is the kingdom of heaven. Blessed are you when people insult you and persecute you, and falsely say all kinds of evil against you because of Me. Rejoice and be glad, for your reward in heaven is great; for in the same way they persecuted the prophets who were before you" (Matt. 5:10–12).

- "Who is there to harm you if you prove zealous for what is good? But even if you should suffer for the sake of righteousness, you are blessed. AND DO NOT FEAR THEIR INTIMIDATION, AND DO NOT BE IN DREAD, but sanctify Christ as Lord in your hearts, always being ready to make a defense to everyone who asks you to give an account for the hope that is in you, yet with gentleness and respect; and keep a good conscience so that in the thing in which you are slandered, those who disparage your good behavior in Christ will be put to shame. For it is better, if God should will it so, that you suffer for doing what is right rather than for doing what is wrong" (1 Pet. 3:13–17).

- "Lord, look at their threats, and grant it to Your bond-servants to speak Your word with all confidence, while You extend Your hand to heal, and signs and wonders take place through the name of Your holy servant Jesus" (Acts 4:29–30).

- "Weeping may last for the night, But a shout of joy comes in the morning" (Ps. 30:5).

- "Who comforts us in all our affliction so that we will be able to comfort those who are in any affliction with the comfort with which we ourselves are comforted by God. . . . For we do not want you to be unaware, brethren, of our affliction which occurred in Asia, that we were burdened excessively, beyond our strength, so that we despaired even of life. . . . so that we would not trust in ourselves, but in God who raises the dead" (2 Cor. 1:4, 8–9).

God is busy doing a work in you and me. We each have our own package of trials and disappointments. They've been designed by our heavenly Father to make us better people. We don't exactly choose difficulties. The darker the night, the brighter the light.

Former Israeli Prime Minister Golda Meir once said, "One cannot and must not try to erase the past merely because it does not fit the present."[5]

Regarding your past hardships, consider this, "I have never met a strong person with an easy past. Be proud of your scars and that you're still standing. Strong people are strong because their past was NOT EASY."[6] How is it we think we would be an exception to every rule? Even our Lord God had to hang on a tree until His death, suffering more than words can describe.

With an onslaught of hardships, we have the power through the Holy Spirit to face these realities head-on and make necessary choices to look hard to find all the positives possible to dwell on. Carefully refuse to wallow in the pains. The positives are there if we'll make that choice.

Remember again the advice Isaiah 55:8–11, "'For My thoughts are not your thoughts, Nor are your ways My ways,' declares the LORD. 'For as the heavens are higher than the earth, So are My ways higher than your ways And My thoughts than your thoughts. . . . So will My word be which goes forth from My mouth; It will not return to Me empty, Without accomplishing what I desire, And without succeeding in the purpose for which I sent it.'"

Study Questions for Chapter 6: Setbacks and Trials

1. What must I do to prepare to face trials? See Ephesians 6:11, 13.

2. Share some of your frustrating setbacks in life.

3. What does the Bible say about our being burdened excessively and what is the purpose of these extensive trials? See 2 Corinthians 1:8–10.

4. Name some of our admonitions to follow when getting into a lot of anxiety. Identify the verbs of action in 1 Peter 5:6–10.

5. How is God's healing power for brokenness demonstrated in Joshua 1:5–9?

6. Again, why do we have to undergo trials as stated in 1 Corinthians 10:11–13?

7. When your foes are trampling upon you all day long, what are you supposed to do? See Psalm 56:3.

8. To avoid withering away during your trials, how does Psalm 1:1–2 explain that you will be blessed instead?

9. Name biblical characters who had issues to deal with. How did God use them?

10. Write down and then read aloud passages you need to place in your mental file drawers to rehearse what benefits you will experience through the many trials you face.

11. Rehearse what God does for you and is to you during your troubled times.

12. How are God's ways higher than ours? See Isaiah 55:8–11. What does He tell us?

7

Real Stories of Responses to Tough Trials

Putting our trust in God and not circumstances grants true security to the believer in Christ. It's a given we are going to experience trouble in this life. Second Timothy 3:12 even says, "all who want to live in a godly way in Christ Jesus will be persecuted." Just what we wanted to hear . . . Yet trials definitely give us opportunity to grow with our proper responses.

Granted, we don't like hardships. Some are much more intense than others and cannot be compared with someone else's. One of our African friends was in our home while studying theology in this country. After his dedicated five years of advanced studies here, he returned to his homeland to minister to his people. His and his family's lives have been in imminent danger because it's not popular to be an outward Bible-believing person where they live. Besides experiencing the hardship of malaria, they watch the attacks from enemies on all sides, attacking, kidnapping, raping, and killing. Thousands are being forced to run for cover, being displaced from their homes. Our friends are anything but feeling safe. Do they feel hope? Their mindset in words is, "Our only hope is God who is our shield and protector." Is what is happening wrong and unacceptable—yes. They express being profoundly grateful for the prayers and support of God's people. More words from them, "the Lord leads us in this project of faith." They sign their message, "Remain blessed," and their names. What a response from those under extreme danger.

Years ago there were five missionaries killed in Ecuador by the Auca Indians. There have been books and a movie made about this horrific story. Months before this happened Nate Saint, one of those killed, flew my family into a missionary training center in southern Mexico, so we got to appreciate his life personally.

Then, years later, Nate's son Steve was in our home while in town to speak at our church. Steve traveled with Mincaye, one of the Indians who killed Nate, Steve's dad. This horrible story of Nate being killed turned into a remarkable redemption story. Mincaye came to know Jesus and the family literally took him into their home, calling him grandpa even. This reality displays the incredibly positive response after such extreme hardship this family had to endure. The response showed forgiveness to an extent many of us haven't experienced. Such a positive response brought restoration, while having to lose Nate from his earthly time here. That story of redemption is displayed in our front room where a pig's tooth necklace Mincaye presented us hangs over the cross on the wall.

My husband's year in Viet Nam was used by God to get his attention during times of possible death. Stu responded to his Lord and chose to discontinue his personal plan for self-fulfillment but follow what he saw to be God's chosen plan for his and our future. Thus, he resigned his regular Army commission and came home to start seminary. It didn't matter that he gave up a full scholarship to any college or university with a full captain's pay while pursuing theology training. It was a new mindset.

My husband gets a lot of mail from readers who have read his books to tell him of life changes they have made. One young man who failed high school freshman English twice, and barely got out of high school as a two-time senior wrote of his redemption story. While in the Army he ended up listening to a speech my husband was giving at his post. He didn't want to be there but he came, listened, and the message lay dormant for some time, even though it had sunk in deeply. He decided to get my husband's books, which led him on a path of change after being lost.

During that "lost season," he had responsible jobs, being a federal agent, selected by the Secret Service, yet ended up in jail. There he had a lot of time to rethink his life process. He's read hundreds of books and pursued degrees in theology and pastoral ministry with a 4.0 GPA. He became ordained and licensed by a national Christian ministry and by the grace of God is giving sermons, teaching, baptizing, and discipling many. He now says he must live for his Lord and Savior, doing his heavenly Father's work here. From being a lost soul to now being saved is this man's greatest blessing.

I have many close friends right now with stage four cancer and several with massive strokes that have changed their lives. These are major trials, which require a lot of evaluation as to how best to respond. Not exactly what each had planned. We can learn from others as we observe their responses.

Many of you have read some of the books on the market by Randy Alcorn. His wife, Nanci, wrote a blog titled, *My Cancer Is God's Servant*. These special friends of ours say this:

> We haven't given up and we prayed for complete healing again tonight as we have every night for nearly four years. But neither are we presuming to tell God what He must do just because we want it. *He is God,* we are not. Immediate short-term healing is not a certainty, but ultimate long-term healing is woven into the gospel. It is the blood-bought promise of Jesus! . . . We don't know, and neither do the doctors, what's ahead of us. We are only finite but praise God we know personally the infinite One who's in charge of the universe and who lovingly supervises our lives! When we received the worst news, we said, "God has been with us in all this, and He still is."[1]

They proceeded to talk about how gracious and kind God has been and how they sensed His presence. They knew the seriousness of the diagnosis; they did not live in denial and definitely shed tears along the way, but in it all by God's grace they maintained a contagiously upbeat mindset. We can learn from this God-honoring response. Thank you for teaching all of us, Randy and Nanci.

The Alcorns clung to Scripture, such as Proverbs 19:21, "Many plans are in a person's heart, but the advice of the LORD will stand." Their journal in November 2021 said, "Along with the hardship, God will bring us times of joy and delight even in the challenges of these treatments. He's done it before, He will do it again. . . . If the time comes when God seems ready to take either of us home we will accept that." Other Scripture they leaned on were John 10:28, "I give them eternal life, and they will never perish; and no one will snatch them out of My hand" and Revelation 21:4, "and He will wipe away every tear from their eyes; and there will no longer be any death; there will no longer be any mourning, or crying, or pain."

We can all benefit from Nanci's words about her devastating cancer diagnosis:

> A cure is no longer in my medical playbook. However, God's playbook overrides all others and we continue to ask God to heal me if that is His will. We trust Him completely." She goes on, "I have felt God's presence, His steadfast love, supporting strength, abiding peace, and tender mercy throughout my illness. A few days ago, Randy and I were discussing the invitation from Jesus in John 15:9 for us to abide in his love. Randy explained that meant to make our abode in or to take up residence in and be at home in the love of Jesus. That is where I have been living! And it has caused me to trust Him in every detail of my life. He will always have my best interests in mind even if I don't understand it here and now.[2]

Randy and Nanci pointed others to this verse for how they viewed their trial, 2 Corinthians 4:18, "We look not at the things which are seen, but at the things which are not seen; for the things which are seen are temporal, but the things which are not seen are eternal." May we think and respond likewise in times of distress. Take some time to let all this sink in. This is huge.

After Nanci did pass into the presence of Jesus, Randy continues to expound upon all the Scriptures they spoke of earlier. He believes that God has all things in His plan as Randy humanly misses his dear bride more than is easy to describe.

We can learn from watching dear ones who have experienced the death of a family member. Consider this response from our friend and coworker, Paul Norquist. In a totally shocking experience, Paul's wife, Michelle, was found having already entered heaven after her taking a walk. Paul said only twelve hours after her death, "The grief and shock are almost insurmountable. But God's grace will match it . . . God is good and worthy of our trust. I have a heart filled with gratitude for the 34 ½ years I got to be married to her. Heaven just got a little sweeter for me."[3] How many of us can have such perspective?

We all followed the story of Elizabeth Smart who was a sexual slave for some time. As she got out of this terrible and evil situation, she realized she wanted to be at peace with her past and take her power back. She said she wanted "no power over me. Bad things don't have to define us. . . .What defines you is how you react. Your past does not dictate your future. . . . I was kidnapped but not powerless." Her story is widely told how she is overcoming trauma.[4] Is your past dictating your future?

Another friend, Jay McKinney, who at age forty-six (diagnosed at age thirty-eight), faced his death from cancer and provided all his observers wisdom from above to overcome through it all. There is so much to learn and mirror as one takes their insights from the Scriptures in how to view trials, big or small. Regarding his response to imminent death, "It means you're growing and learning, and taking 100% responsibility for your life. It means you keep choosing grace and not shame, progress over perfection. It means you're not done, and the best of you toward others is yet to come."[5] Wow, what insight and maturity as Jay did enter heaven praising God still.

More friends with the same outlook are quoting all those same verses you've seen above and are speaking to all of us observers with reminders of God's hand in our lives during this season. My friend, Janice Bramwell, speaks of her husband Joel's massive stroke and how it happened so unexpectedly. Life was going on heartily. Joel's life involved a large physical experience with running, hiking, and biking besides a business world of busy schedules.

There was no suspicion of a major life change lurking around the corner for them. Janice relates the mindset God would desire saying, "The story God has for my life and my husband's is written and planned by a God who knows all and always wants our good. This story is not mine and it's not my husband's; it's God's story of reminding us that nothing, nothing can separate us from His love."[6] Such an example for us to imitate.

Janice's Joel did have a second stroke and passed into heaven. Her comments are: "And now he's finally home. His happiest day ever and my saddest. Yet Jesus truly binds our broken hearts with cords of hope—hope that someday I will see him again." She quotes Rev. 21:4, "And God will wipe away every tear from their eyes; there shall be no more death, nor sorrow, or crying. There shall be no more pain, for the former things have passed away."

A lifelong friend of ours from childhood, Dave and his wife, Debbie Jongeward, came to visit Joel and Janice Bramwell before Joel died, having spent quality ministry time together years prior. Dave has been going through treatment for his stage four brain cancer and these two couples were sharing on a very intimate common level of life and death. Dave and Joel voiced how they have a sense of peace and trust through it all. Even before the latest life-changing diagnosis, and from another shocking life event, Dave shared a verse that had become even more poignant. Psalm 18:39, "For You have encircled me with strength for battle; You have forced those who rose up against me to bow down under me."

Dave said, "God prepared my heart to rely upon his strength no matter how difficult the journey or battle ahead. . . . I have total peace with God and within myself. . . . It is well with my soul! I totally surrendered to God again at the beginning of this journey, so I have total freedom to just trust God for His timing and results!! I'm NOT in charge . . . I'm NOT in control . . . that's a very freeing feeling!! I'd rather trust God with my life anyway than myself." Dave knows that his kind of cancer gives him only a 25 percent chance to live a year. He says, "I know I have eternal life already, so now it's just a matter of how much life this side of eternity."[7] Such strong examples to follow. Later Dave did receive a total clean bill of health.

Numerous friends who surround us have physical limitations. Some march on doing their best while others are bitter and complain continually. With the latter, do they need you to know how miserable they are? One friend who cannot walk gets around in a motorized chair and has special provisions in his vehicle to help him drive everywhere. Nobody who knows him thinks of him as disabled. He goes everywhere that everybody else goes, and you never hear him talking about it either. He tries everything, like skiing. He has his special equipment to sit while going down the mountain. Nothing stops Jerry Gilmore. How about us? Do we have that attitude? It's a mindset.

Some people lose everything they have, maybe it's their family in death, accident, or disaster of some kind. Some lose through tough investments. Let's look at Job in the Bible. Job was "blameless, upright, fearing God and turning away from evil" (Job 1:1). His possessions were extensive in every way and his family was large. Numerous disasters took place and wiped it all away. Even his friends rejected him with betrayals. His health left him feeling his life was futile. Scripture tells how he went through much lamenting. So what was his response through it all? "Then Job got up, tore his robe, and shaved his head; then he fell to the ground and worshiped. He said, 'Naked I came from my mother's womb, and naked I shall return there. The LORD gave and the LORD has taken away. Blessed be the name of the LORD.' Despite all this, Job did not sin, nor did he blame God" (1:20–22).

The results of so much hardship doesn't often end like Job's story did, yet it's a pleasure to read what happened: Job 42:10 says, "The LORD also restored the fortunes of Job when he prayed for his friends, and the LORD increased double all that Job had." The story goes on to tell how the Lord blessed the latter days of Job more than the beginning.

Although Job had a wild pilgrimage, let's look at his good responses to the extreme problems he experienced:

- "But as for me, I would seek God, And I would make my plea before God, Who does great and unsearchable things, Wonders without number" (5:8–9).

- "But it is still my comfort, And I rejoice in unsparing pain, That I have not denied the words of the Holy One" (6:10).
- "Teach me, and I will be silent; And show me how I have done wrong. How painful are honest words!" (6:24–25).

I challenge you to pursue "extra credit" in seeing how Job responded positively to severe circumstances and read the following passages: Job 13:15; 14:15; 19:25; 23:10; 33:4; 34:10; and 42:5–6. Job 42:2 sums it up, "I know that You can do all things, And that no plan is impossible for You." Bless this man's heart.

The wife of Todd Beamer, the well-known 9/11 hero, tells her audiences after losing her husband that trusting God's plans completely has never been more important than now. Lisa Beamer quotes God's Word: "Who has known the mind of the Lord? Or who became His counselor? Who has first given to Him that it would be paid back to Him?" (Rom. 11:34–35). Their children were young when they lost their daddy and she wanted to equip the kids with "a strong vision and capacity for character, faith and courage which makes a difference in our world."

This hero's wife says circumstances have changed dramatically but that her God has not—and neither has her perspective. She keeps drawing attention back to God, who uniquely prepared both she and her husband "for such a time as this" (Esth. 4:14). She often quotes another Scripture to show her perspective, Genesis 50:20, "You meant evil against me, but God meant it for good in order to bring about this present result, to keep many people alive."[8]

A rebellious unnamed woman was written up in *Moody* about how her mom had faced serious illnesses and marital problems and then she faced her own emptiness and discontentment in her marriage. Scripture had never been pertinent to her, but her mom pursued the sharing of God's Word with her in her depressed state of mind and then things changed. She came to realize that happiness wasn't what she was searching for—it was Jesus Christ. With her new realizations she knew she had a longing to know God. She now has joy exceeding happiness.[9]

When my boys were young they liked to ride their bikes down the street. Great, that is a good thing for boys to do. But, there happened to be some troubled brothers who would literally shoot my guys with their BB guns when they went by. That was not going to work.

Of course we weren't going to have any more rides going down past that house now. Returning fire with fire only sets you up for some more issues. It seems a bit crazy, but I suggested we take them a plate of cookies to be positive rather than hammering them with threats. My boys had no interest in being nice to these guys who were trying to hurt them. They just said, "we'll throw those things in their face." In the end, we stayed away, and no cookies were presented or thrown.

We don't have to look far to find marriages breaking up. The differences between men and women are written in the textbooks. Yet, many don't have this basic understanding down. So, when one partner is so totally different and the other cannot tolerate or accept these differences, it's pretty easy to just pack your bags and decide that there is greener grass on the other side of the fence. It's a lifetime of making positive responses to either differences or the trials you encounter together that will decide what the future will look like. When you have to encounter hard things together, do you just quit and take your marbles to the next game because you didn't get your way?

Physical disabilities and medical traumas grip our souls for a response. It's not easy. A young man named Steve Sharp, lost both arms in a hay baling accident. Bless his heart, he was trying to get the hay out of the baler and all of a sudden, it kicked on and sucked both arms in. Unimaginable trauma. His attitude and response was indeed out of the box. The description of it all is more than I want to share for our not getting sick. After a very bloody description and time that would pass, this eighteen-year-old's response during his recovery was remarkable. "Once you get to where you can do something, it gets easier and easier." Before long everyone agreed that he was merely unusually resilient and stoic for one so young. The newspaper article about his story was quoted like this, "By all appearances, Sharp is a living testament to 17th century essayist Francis Bacon's observation that the 'virtue of adversity is fortitude.'" When asked what profession in life he might follow, he said, "I'm still looking around; I'll find something I can do. It shouldn't be too much of a problem." The word *surrender* never even crossed his mind.[9]

Many stories come to my mind with this subject and we could go on for a long time with them. This next story coming here stands out as extra unique. Both partners probably felt they were putting up with things they didn't like. The wife had been praying for her husband for twenty-eight years as she observed his total focus in life to be self-fulfilled and then his becoming the CEO of one of the largest companies in our country. His life was anything but Christian and she was a totally serious student of the Bible, giving herself to being all that God had designed.

We learned about this marriage because the man wrote my husband, including a one hundred dollar bill in the letter, thanking Stu for his book that his wife gave to him. He said it had been used to change his life. He went on to say that everybody in his realm, family and business associates, neighbors and friends all were telling him how they were observing a major change. He had come to know Jesus. Furthermore, he wanted to take us out to dinner to say a big thank you. We did live 2,300 miles apart, but we happened to be making a trip there for our son Kent's (and Carolyn's) wedding. Sure enough, we got to meet this couple and had a very fun dinner and sharing time. So many positive responses to a hard story. God is at work for all of us.

Another story—this time dealing with financial repercussions—is of a friend who made a large investment, including the equity of their home. From all the outward signs, that investment should have had a smart and helpful ending. Well, it didn't. He lost their very nice home and many of their prized possessions. Did that stop the productivity of that person? No. He had a mindset to get up and go again, but not in that kind of investing. A few years later, he has a new home and it is almost paid off. Asking that person about whether he has a lot of bad days, he says, "No, they are a waste of time." He had a mindset to never give up. No complaining, just do it.

We can be better people on the other side of trouble, depending on our mindset. How are you doing with yours?

People with a mindset to overcome give us encouragement to always have hope. A skier named Diana Golden lost her right leg to cancer. She was considered one of the best ski racers, among men and women, able-bodied or not. She garnered twenty-nine world and national disabled skiing championships and an Olympic gold medal along the way. "I went for a world title," saying, "I want to do it for me, 100%, not as a disabled athlete. I was doing it with a passion for excellence." She helped others with disabilities until her death in 2013. "You have to keep knocking. It's slow. We respect ourselves. Anger doesn't help. It just eats away at you."[10]

Do we choose to make the most of our situations? A nicely dressed and well-poised ninety-two-year-old woman who had just lost her husband was accompanied to her new residence. After waiting in the lobby until the room was ready, she was told about the details of this new place. Her response: "I love it." The helper said, "But you haven't seen it." Although this fashionably dressed woman with careful makeup was legally blind, she continued, "That doesn't have anything to do with it. *Happiness is something you decide ahead of time. It's a decision.*"

Positive, redemptive stories are all around us and we should be encouraged by the changing powers our God allows. Our oldest son, Kent, went off to Oxford in England for a second advanced degree, fulfilling a junior high dream of his. He immediately met a young woman named Carolyn who was on a track that displayed an anti-God pursuit. He showed her how God loved her, and she learned a lot as she searched the Scriptures. Over time she bowed her knee and asked God to forgive her sin and became a child of the King. It's a long story but she ended up writing a book about it all. *Surprised by Oxford* tells this story of redemption that displays God's handiwork from her broken life—it is now a movie as well.

It's helpful to review positive stories because the negative ones are far and wide. When we see how others go through hard times and make choices that can benefit all in the end we are stimulated to go and do likewise. Life is hard and things don't go well in so many cases. If we slip into the anger mode and start intimidating those around us with mockery, blaming, and with raised voices, everybody loses.

We are all writing our life stories in real time. Let's make those smart choices so generations to come have models to emulate. Decide now about how you'll respond during your next trial so others can receive hope from all that God brought you through.

Study Questions for Chapter 7: Real Stories of Responses to Tough Trials

1. What is your response to 2 Timothy 3:12?

2. Discuss the faith of the various people featured in the stories in this chapter. See 2 Corinthians 4:18; Philippians 1:23; Revelation 21:4.

3. In the midst of trouble, what are we encouraged to do? See John 15:9.

4. See Psalm 18:39 to see how God prepares us.

5. What are some of the response comments we can learn from as we find ourselves in trials?

6. Job experienced extreme loses. It will be instructive to our souls to rehearse Job's positive responses. (He did have negative ones too.) See Job 5:8–9; 6:10; 6:24; 13:15.

7. What can we learn from Genesis 50:20?

8. Discuss some wilderness experiences of yours or friends or stories from this chapter and how we best learn from them.

9. Interact over this statement, "Putting our trust in God and not circumstances grants true security to the believer in Christ."

10. Write out Romans 5:3 and 4 and consider memorizing this.

11. Talk about the perspective you are gaining after observing various saints' responses to Scripture.

12. Reflect personally and perhaps in the group how you want to get rid of your anger, bitterness, and unforgiveness from holding hostage both yourself and the people who have done you wrong, freeing you to be all God would have for you.

How Will the Bible
Help Me Anyway?

O n our bathroom wall hangs a plaque reminding us that God is going to handle all our issues today, so we can just hand them all over to Him. How is it we think we have to do it all ourselves? Well, we do possess a Bible and it definitely gives us God's direction if we'll merely consult it and see how God helps us, and in detail. Our Bibles are like lifelines our God is throwing out to us to save us from drowning in the midst of life's confusion, hardships, and issues.

If you have unhealed traumas in your life, they can be resolved by getting to KNOW and then TRUSTING the big God we learn about in the written WORD OF GOD, the Bible. He is your source to handle anything. He lavishes you with grace, affirmation, unconditional love, and direction like nowhere else. Your answers lie here so you can shed the weights that might be taking you down. Walk away from all the disinformation Satan would have you believe and walk into the light that will make your path straight. Let's enable the God-factor agenda to prevail that avoids the kidnapping of our brains into thinking other than in God's perfect plan for us. It's a choice we get to make—to search for this or not.

Like anything in life, we want to know why we should do whatever. When we know the reasons why, we're more motivated to follow through. God's Word gives us the "why" and the "how." The psalmist in 119:93 says, "I will never forget your precepts, For by them, You *have revived me*." Proverbs 4:13 says, "Take hold of instruction; do not let go. Guard her, for *she is your life*." Proverbs 4:6, "Do not abandon her, and *she will guard you*. Love her, and *she will watch over you*."

When you visit London and ride the Tube, you hear the recording as you step aboard to "mind the gap." Better pay attention or those gaps will cause you dismay. And, in the movie *Rocky*, he states, "I've got gaps, she's got gaps, we all have gaps." When something is missing in our lives, we have gaps. When we realize this lack, we will quit depending on our natural selves and come to realize the Bible is going to help fill in the gaps. It will lift our eyes to the meaningful life here and give directions for an eternal home in heaven later.

Let's look at Hosea 14:9, "Whoever is wise, let him understand these things; whoever is discerning, let him know them. For the ways of the LORD are right, And the righteous will walk in them, but wrongdoers will stumble in them."

We don't like to give up things unless we *know* it's necessary. Years ago, one of my friends changed their family's eating habits because the dad ended up having much of his stomach removed. His life really turned around for the better with all the changes made to his eating plan. Another friend had similar health issues, so I asked her to share all of her research on the subject if I gathered a few people to listen.

One thing led to another, and it turned out to be a three-night presentation of two hours each, with a hundred thirty-three people present! I asked her if she would write down specific reasons why people need to stay away from white sugar, among other things. That sugar paper ended up being a thirteen-page, single-space research project to pass out to everybody. I needed to have some detailed reasons if I was to take my health seriously and stay away from white sugar.

So why do I need to read the Bible and what good will that do me in the middle of my busy world? Acts 26:18 speaks to that, "to open their eyes so that they may turn from darkness to light and from the dominion of Satan to God, that they may receive forgiveness of sins and an inheritance among those who have been sanctified by faith in Me." Let's look at Ephesians 5:13 and 17, "All things become visible when they are exposed by the light, for everything that becomes visible is light. . . . do not be foolish, but understand what the will of the Lord is."

In days past I enjoyed selling real estate. The key factor in buying a home is to consider three things: location, location, location. Regarding this subject of how the Bible is going to help me, the three reasons you need for knowing your Bible are: foundation, foundation, foundation. If you don't have a foundation, life isn't going to work. Second Corinthians 5:17 says, "If anyone is in Christ, this person is a new creation; the old things passed away; behold, *new things have come.*" Part of that foundation is expressed in John 8:32, "You will know the truth, and *the truth will set you free.*" More foundation is expressed here: "the one who does the will of God *continues to live forever*" (1 John 2:17).

You may be one of those people who doesn't see much need to read a Bible. After getting a better understanding of why you need it, I would hope you will have found new purpose for this process. You've got to go through a process to get the product. To cultivate a new habit of reading the Word, I want to show you from Scripture why and how you are going to benefit.

First, the Bible is your way to God. "In the beginning was the Word, and the Word was with God, and the Word was God" (John 1:1). Here you will develop a spiritual understanding. That will come when you become a child of God—by asking for forgiveness for your natural-born sin nature and, by an act of will, inviting Christ into your life. You go from being the natural man, born that way, to being a child of God, supernaturally. Let's look how 1 Corinthians 2:12–16 explains this in part:

Now we have received, not the spirit of the world, but the Spirit who is from God, so that we may know the things freely given to us by God. We also speak these things, not in words taught by human wisdom, but in those taught by the Spirit, combining spiritual thoughts with spiritual words. But a natural person does not accept the things of the Spirit of God, for they are foolishness to him; and he cannot understand them, because they are spiritually discerned. But the one who is spiritual discerns all things, yet he himself is discerned by no one. For who has known the mind of the Lord, that he will instruct Him? But we have the mind of Christ.

So then, we get to know this God by learning to know His Word. The more we get to know our Bibles, the better we get to know our God. It's simple math, two plus two equals four. We can say we wish we knew the Bible better, yet our human nature pretty much keeps us busy doing everything else than pursuing God. Other things seem more important in our busyness. We can all relate to that. The Bible speaks to our tendency to stay away, confronts us, and tells us why to choose differently: "'Awake sleeper, And arise from the dead, And Christ will shine on you.' So then, be careful how you walk, not as unwise men but be wise, making the most of your time, because the days are evil. Therefore do not be foolish, but understand what the will of the Lord is" (Eph. 5:14–17).

I wish I knew the Bible better

It's our human nature to want the benefits in life without doing what is required of us to enjoy them.

From the Scriptures, below you will see the benefits of spending time in the Bible. You first see the conditions necessary and then the results we can enjoy. There is responsibility needed before we receive the privilege. Let's understand the process we must choose to go through in order to enjoy the product.

Stipulation	Benefits
Condition necessary	Result
IF this is true	*THEN* this can happen
Responsibility required	Privilege enjoyed
The process	The product

If You	*Then*
Psalm 1:2–4	
• ***delight*** in the Law of the LORD and you ***meditate*** on it day and night	You will be like a tree planted by streams of water: • yielding fruit • leaf not withering • prospering in whatever you do • not blowing away like chaff
Proverbs 2:1–5, 9–11	
• ***Receive*** my words	You will discern the fear of the LORD
• ***Treasure*** my commandments	You will discover the knowledge of God
• ***Make your ear attentive*** to wisdom	You will discern righteousness and justice
• ***Incline*** your heart to understanding	Wisdom will enter your heart
• ***Cry*** for discernment	From His mouth comes understanding
• ***Lift up*** your voice for understanding	He stores up sound wisdom (for you)
• ***Seek*** understanding as you do silver	He is a shield for you, guarding paths of justice
• ***Search*** for her as for hidden treasures	He preserves you; discretion guards you
• ***Are upright***	You will discern equity and every good course
• ***Walk in integrity, guarding***	Knowledge will be the paths of justice pleasant to your soul
• ***Are His godly ones***	Discretion will guard you
James 1:25	
• But the one who ***looks intently*** at the perfect law	This man shall be blessed in what he does
• Continues in ***it***, ***not*** having become a ***forgetful hearer***, but ***an active doer***	

If You	*Then*
Hebrews 5:13–14	
• *Are practicing [your minds]* in the word of righteousness (solid food is for the mature), that is *(exercising* your minds)	Our senses are trained to distinguish between good and evil.
Proverbs 3:19–26	
• *do not escape* from your sight	They will be life to your neck. You will walk securely and your foot will not stumble
• *comply with* sound wisdom and discretion	When you lie down your sleep will be sweet
• *Do not be afraid* of sudden danger	The LORD will be your confidence and will keep your foot from being caught
2 Peter 3:17–18	
• *Be on your guard*, *grow in grace* and *knowledge* of our Lord and Savior Jesus Christ	So that you are not carried away by the error of unscrupulous people, and lose your own firm commitment
John 15:7	
• *Remain in me* and *my words remain in you*	Ask whatever you will and it shall be done for you
1 John 1:7	
• *Walk in the light* as He is in the Light	We have fellowship with one with another
Ephesians 5:13	
• *Exposed by the light* (Our being in the Word)	all things become visible
Philippians 1:9–10	
• *Overflowing more and more* in real knowledge and all discernment	You will be able to discover things that are excellent

Isn't it interesting how we want all the benefits without doing the work to get them. Let's keep looking at Scripture to grasp what difference it'll make when we spend time in our Bibles. It can truly change lives.

Benefits Available to Us with Expectations from God for Us

Psalm 78:4	*tell the generation to come* the praises of the LORD and His power and His wondrous works that He has done.
Psalm 78:6	that the generation to come would know, the children yet to be born that they *would arise and tell them to their children*
Psalm 78:7	that they *would put their confidence in God and not forget the works of God*
Proverbs 4:13	*Take hold of instruction; do not let go. Guard her,* for she is your life.
Romans 15:4	For whatever was written in earlier times was written for our instruction, that *through perseverance and the encouragement of the Scriptures*, we might have hope.
2 Peter 1:19–20	And so we have the prophetic word made more sure to which you do well to *pay attention* as to a lamp shining in a dark place.
Deuteronomy 5:29	If only they *had such heart in them, to fear Me, and keep all my commandments always*, so that it would go well with them and with their sons forever
Psalm 102:18–22	This will be written for the generation to come; *that a people yet to be created may praise the Lord*. For He looked down from His holy height . . . to hear, to set free . . . *that people may tell of the name of the LORD in Zion . . . to serve the Lord.*
1 Corinthians 10:11–12	Now these things happened to them as an example, and they were written for our instruction, upon whom the ends of the ages have come. Therefore let the one who thinks he stands *watch out that he does not fall.*
Proverbs 4:20–22	*Pay attention to my words; Incline your ear to my sayings. They are not to escape from your sight; Keep them in the midst of your heart;* for they are life to those who find them, and healing to all their body.

What Can I Learn by Reading the Bible?

- Think like God thinks
- Respond like God responds
- Act like God, mirror His likeness
- Plan how He would
- Prioritize like He does

- Live in light of who God is and what He does for me
- Capitalize on my blessings, not others' weaknesses
- Become equipped to do life
- Avoid compartmentalizing

- Possess wisdom like God offers
- Trust through hardships

- Gain perspective; want more and more of Jesus
- Hate sin and be angry at it
- Luxuriate in His presence; anticipate heaven with pleasure
- Accept difficulties for my growth

- Rehearse God's forever design
- Stop dividing my mind (Phil. 4:6)

- Know how vast God is
- Love like God loves
- Become more like Him

- Make choices like He would
- Know Him and the responsibilities He gives me

- Understand my need to obey, follow, keep and why
- Evaluate accurately His design

- Personalize the facts
- Run from victimization and narcissism
- Find hope like never before
- Release strongholds of negativism and sin

- Be energized with godliness

- See discipline in a positive light
- Stop negative behaviors that destroy
- Experience the better way; appreciate being God's child

- Enjoy immersion in God's plan
- Live like the Bible is true and tell others

You are going to see purpose like never before.
You'll want more and more and more.
You need help? You've got it.
Your eyes will be opened to the treasures in God's Word.

Psalm 23 (KJV)

The LORD is my Shepherd—*that's* **RELATIONSHIP!**

I shall not want—*that's* **SUPPLY!**

He maketh me to lie down in green pastures—*that's* **REST!**

He leadeth me beside the still waters—*that's* **REFRESHMENT!**

He restoreth my soul—*that's* **PROVISION!**

He leadeth me in the paths of righteousness—*that's* **GUIDANCE!**

For his name's sake—*that's* **PURPOSE!**

Yea, though I walk through the valley of the shadow of death—
    that's **TESTING!**

I will fear no evil—*that's* **PROTECTION!**

For thou art with me—*that's* **FAITHFULNESS!**

Thy rod and thy staff they comfort me—*that's* **DISCIPLINE!**

Thou preparest a table before me in the presence of mine ene-
    mies—*that's* **HOPE!**

Thou anointest my head with oil—*that's* **CONSECRATION!**

My cup runneth over—*that's* **FULFILLMENT!**

Surely goodness and mercy shall follow me all the days of my
    life—*that's* **BLESSING!**

And I shall dwell in the house of the LORD forever—*that's*
    SECURITY!

Purpose will be discovered in the promises. They go hand in hand. Abraham in Hebrews 11:8 is on display, "By faith Abraham, when he was called, obeyed by **going** out to a place which he was to receive for an inheritance; and he went out, **not knowing** where he was going." God gives to us, asks obedience of us, and rewards us. The Bible gives us everything we need to make life happen well.

I hope you'll do your personal study of the promises of God. These precious gifts are what you can cling to forever. They will encourage you daily and give you assurance of life eternal.

Grasping the value and importance of God's Word reminds us this is the master design for life. All decisions and pursuits should start here. This is the blueprint; God is the architect. Revelation 22:13 tells us, "I am the Alpha and the Omega, the first and the last, the beginning and the end." He created it all and knows how things work best. There will be true order. Purpose is realized. Jeremiah 6:16 says, "Stand by the ways and see and ask for the ancient paths, Where the good way is, and walk in it; Then **you will find rest for your souls**."

Consider the construction worker trying to build a house without a plan. If the foundation is not solid and the thousands of details needed to be followed are not adhered to, there will be disasters. *Thank You, Lord for giving us Your Word to know how to do life.*

When you get serious about your pursuit of God through the Bible, and activate His designs for you, the description of the tree in Psalm 1:3 will be like you "planted by streams of water, Which yields its fruit in its season, And its leaf does not wither; And in whatever he does, he prospers." All that fruit will be displaying how you are overcoming a gloom-and-doom mindset. The fruit you are producing displays confidence, empowerment, purpose, wisdom, direction, and more.

Strong roots/healthy fruits

As you choose to make God's Word personal, you'll overcome that tendency to be caught in the gravity flow downward. You'll overcome wrong thinking. Instead, your Bible **will equip you to rise above**. It is your life instruction book. It's the ultimate item we receive or purchase. You have PERSONAL access to the real source of strength and power—and THAT'S why God gave us His Word.

Study Questions for Chapter 8: How Will the Bible Help Me Anyway?

1. What revives us? See Psalm 119:93. Is this true of you?

2. What does God tell us to do? See Proverbs 4:13; 4:6.

3. Have you ever wished you knew the Bible better? So then, are we activating that wish by doing something for that pursuit? What are we allowing to stop that?

4. Are we aware of how full or empty our mental file drawers are to know the mind of our Lord? (It does take time and dedication as a matter of importance.)

5. When you know the truth, what happens? See John 8:32.

6. What is the relationship between God and His Word? See John 1:1.

7. Looking at Proverbs 2:1–5, 9–11, what are our responsibilities? As we do all those things, write out the results we will enjoy. It is extensive.

8. Write out the verbs of action shown in this chapter from many Scriptures given.

9. Rehearse the many benefits listed as you fulfill your commands in the Scriptures presented in this chapter. (If you . . . then . . .)

10. Review the many ways you'll maximize your life from your Bible study as listed in this chapter. (You can be like the healthy tree with roots and fruit.)

11. List the many blessings presented us in Psalm 23, as given in the chapter.

12. See Hebrews 11:8. We see Abraham "going not knowing." Share a new desire you might have to get to know your God better, and proceed to follow Him, "going not knowing."

13. What inspired you most as a life changer in reviewing the principles here?

The God-Factor: The Bottom Line for All of Life

If we have adequate knowledge of the facts, we are prepared to know how to make accurate assessments. Knowledge is not overrated, and knowing God well prepares us with how to think, act, and to know why. So our decisions are only as smart as the information we possess. Therefore, we are going to maximize our understanding of God and pursuing the incorporation of the God-factor into our lives with these pages. God's Word is forever and not outdated, and it's not misinformation as some might want to claim.

This life is inundated with nasty invaders of trouble, and if we fail to understand the God-factor that changes everything, we can simply go down with a sinking ship. Recognizing and acquiring the God-factor allows us the only true power source to overcome. It's the secret for everything and it doesn't have to remain unknown. It is so sad people will try everything except God as their true solution for everything.

The promises He makes will sustain us through everything if we will only claim them. If you have enemies of one kind or another, Psalm 23:5 reminds you how He "prepare[s] a table before me in the presence of my enemies." He cares for us, and we get to exhibit His grace in our lives. He has planned our victory party. He is calling—are you listening?

The Bible speaks to our forever needs. Daniel 11:32 says, "The people who know their God **will be strong and take action**." That's what I want and I know you do too. Romans 8:35, 37–39 reminds us of this incredible promise to us:

> Who will separate us from the love of Christ? Will tribulation, or trouble, or persecution, or famine, or nakedness, or danger, or sword? . . . In all these things we overwhelmingly conquer through Him who loved us. For I am convinced that neither death, nor life, nor angels, nor principalities, nor things present, nor things to come, nor powers, nor height, nor depth, nor any other created thing will be able to separate us from the love of God that is in Christ Jesus our Lord.

Once we ask God into our hearts and lives, we can then have a God-factor in our lives, which produces a totally different outlook about everything. When we have a big God, we can trust Him and not be held hostage by the enormous fear factor. Rehearsing and believing the character of God can change your life. The God-factor allows us to move through those hurdles and over the mountains regardless the dysfunctions and lacks we face on every side. We can recalculate with God's GPS and know He's on our side, helping us all along the way. He is always there and waiting for us to come to Him: "The Lord is good to those who wait for Him, To the person who seeks Him" (Lam. 3:25).

There's such pleasure to develop a mindset after the heart of God. It sets us up to trust and thus avoid the anxiety that can rule every piece of our lives. Really, no more excuses why I must insist on hanging on to my woes. When there are tribulations on every side, we have that steady source to calm the sea and grant perspective. **He** is capable and, frankly, we are not. If you need a weapon to confront chaos, the answer lies with knowing God intimately through His Word. The roadmap is there. The power is there. What more could we ask for? He wants to train your brain to think Godward and not relying on what comes naturally. Recalculating is frequently necessary.

Regardless the minefields we find ourselves in, depending on our allowing the God-factor to prevail provides us the HOPE we desperately need. As we let HOPE be the name of our "game," we don't let public opinion or turbulent circumstances take us down. The injustices we so frequently face will roll off so much more easily. All the stupid stuff surrounding us will not distract us when our Hope-factor rules over it all.

Romans 15:13 speaks it well, "Now may the God of hope fill you with all joy and peace in believing, so that you will abound in hope by the power of the Holy Spirit." We need what God provides for us. Romans 5:5 says, "Hope does not disappoint, because the love of God has been poured out within our hearts through the Holy Spirit who was given to us."

I feel blessed that I had a mom who rehearsed the character of God her entire life. We had no money, or nice things, or living quarters you could invite people to. No fine clothes to be had. I thought my boyfriend's family was rich because they ate meat on Sundays. Vacations of any kind were non-existent. Beyond the voids, for sixteen years or so when my father was home, life was treacherous. When we were without much-needed basics, Mom had a good attitude. When it was dangerous, volatile, and scary, she would talk about how good God is. She memorized probably thousands of verses ever since she was young, so her mental file drawers were full of instant recall material.

Drawing from my reservoir, the Bible

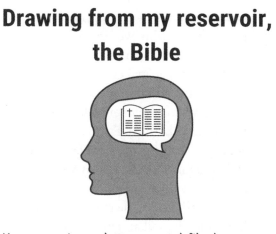

Your reservoir equals your mental file drawers — how complete is your file?

Yes, God is in control of everything (He is sovereign). Nothing takes Him by surprise (He is omniscient). He can handle all situations I face (He is all powerful). Nothing takes Him by surprise (He is immutable). His way is perfect (He is good). He always keeps His promises (He is faithful). He's always fair (He is just). God will meet our needs (He loves us). You can't put our God in a man-made box because He is different (He is holy). (You'll see a repeat of this in a page as a help to remember.)

Maybe you'll find yourself singing the little chorus, "He owns the cattle on a thousand hills"[1] when you find yourself doubting whether God can meet your needs. Or maybe it's a song about being thankful when you find yourself discontent. I would sing to my guys along the way when they were struggling, and they remember those songs well.

To be on top of our game we'd best be looking at life through God's glasses, like we talked about in chapter 1. The God-factor will change things when rehearsing: your circumstances, your upbringing, your problems, your hardships. Our strategy for living definitely needs to be through the lens of our Creator as opposed to letting the natural sway guide our steps.

The God-factor allows us to possess powers that provide the ultimate optimism. It's not that we don't have to experience trials, but we now reach beyond denial with the assurance of our Creator's master design ahead. This brilliance enables a mindset to forge through anything. God is the wind beneath your wings, as the song goes.

God is alive and well. He is not dead nor does He sleep. We take great comfort in knowing He knows everything about us. We must never forget who we are—God's chosen design and loved by our Almighty God. He made us unique to accomplish His purpose. It's the God-factor that makes us confident. God is greater—aren't we fortunate to have this kind of stability in our lives?

So, we must remember God is there. We are not robots, thus we get to choose to LET God work in and through us, or we choose to try and accomplish whatever ourselves, in our flesh. Joshua 24:15 reminds us, "Choose for yourselves today whom you will serve." We have incredible access. When we say we choose to let God do His work in our life, we must then let go of the reins. No more working to control things ourself but rather, be still and know He is God.

Consider 2 Corinthians 12:9–10, "'My grace is sufficient for you, for power is perfected in weakness.' . . . I am delight in weaknesses, in insults, in distresses, in persecutions, in difficulties, in behalf of Christ; for when I am weak, then I am strong." Whew!! The God-factor makes us strong because of His grace being sufficient.

When we get distracted by the complications in life, we need to assess the total picture. In Isaiah 40:28–29 the Israelites were reminded about God's sovereignty amidst all their trials. You have a God-factor, folks. "Do you not know? Have you not heard? The Everlasting God, the LORD, the Creator of the ends of the earth Does not become weary or tired. His understanding is unsearchable. He gives strength to the weary." The question then is, will we wait for the Lord? The promises await you.

Isaiah continues, "Yet those who wait for the LORD Will gain new strength; They will mount up with wings like eagles, They will run and not get tired, They will walk and not become weary" (v. 31). By actively waiting on God to move in our lives, we can then understand Isaiah 55:9: "My ways [are] higher than your ways And My thoughts than your thoughts."

Below are helps for you to grasp the enormity KNOW WHO GOD *IS*.

God Is . . .

LOVE—sacrificial action to meet deep personal needs (1 John 4:7–8; John 3:16; Rom. 5:8; Ps. 48:1)

SOVEREIGN—in control of all things (Ps. 103:19; Isa. 14:24–27; 40:8; Dan. 4:34–35)

OMNIPOTENT—all powerful, can handle all situations (Ps. 62:11; Heb. 1:3; Matt. 6:13)

OMNISCIENT—knows all things, nothing takes Him by surprise (Ps. 44:21; 139:16–17; Acts 2:23)

ALL WISE—His ways are best, perfect (Ps. 104:24; Col. 2:13; Isa. 55:8–9)

OMNIPRESENT—is everywhere present, never leaves us (Ps. 145:18; 46:7, 11; Prov. 15:3)

IMMUTABLE—never changes, never makes a mistake (Mal. 3:6)

FAITHFUL—always keeps His promises (1 Thess. 5:24; 1 John 1:9; Heb. 10:23)

HOLY—different from us (Heb. 7:2; Isa. 6:3; Luke 4:34; Mark 1:24)

JUST—always fair (Rom. 3:26; 7:25); is for me (Psm. 18:30; 55:9; Deut. 32:4)

He is THE:	HE IS:
Door/way (John 10:9, 14:6)	My refuge, fortress, and strength (Psm. 46:1; 62:8; 37:39)
Light (Ps. 27:1; John 8:12)	My sustainer (Ps. 54:4)
Bread of life (John 6:35)	My mediator (Heb. 8:6)
True vine (John 15:1)	My peace (Eph. 2:14)
Alpha & Omega (Rev. 1:8)	My help (Ps. 33:20; John 14:16)
Maker of all (Prov. 22:2)	My rock (Psm. 62:2; 94:22; 95:1)
Image of the invisible God (Col. 1:15)	My protector (Ps. 121:5)
	My advocate (1 John 2:1)
Lord your God (Lev. 18–20)	My firm foundation (1 Cor. 3:11)
Cornerstone (Eph. 2:20)	Pure and right (Ezra 9:15)
	Truthful (John 3:33)
	Kind (Jer. 9:24)
	Eternal (Deut. 33:27)
	Dependable (Ps. 119:138)
	Sufficient (2 Cor. 3:5)
	Victorious (1 Cor. 15:57)
	Immortal (1 Tim. 1:17)
	Merciful (Dan. 9:9)
	Understanding (Prov. 3:19)
	Able (2 Cor. 9:8; Eph. 3:20)
	Good (Psm. 100:5; 145:7)

What are we going to do about knowing we have this big God? Do we **believe** it and **live like this is real and true**? Do we **ask** Him what He would have us be or do? We're told, "But prove yourselves doers of the word, and not merely hears who deceive themselves," (James 1:22). It goes on, in verse 25, if he "has continued in it, not having become a forgetful hearer but an active doer, this person will be blessed in what he does."

With this big a God, we need to get rid of any foreign god we unfortunately allow to take over our thoughts. No renting space of our mind to the wrong people allowed. Gideon needed to be reminded. He was doubting God's work, saying, "The LORD has abandoned us and handed us over to Midian" (Judg. 6:13). The Lord looks at him and says, in 6:14, "Go in this your strength and save Israel from the hand of Midian. Have I not sent you?"

Gideon's insecurity keeps popping in: "How am I to save Israel? Behold, my family is the least in Manasseh, and I am the youngest in my father's house" (v. 15). Then the Lord had to remind him of the strength behind him in this venture: "I will certainly be with you, and you will defeat Midian as one man" (v. 16). Gideon was *almost* confident, but still said in verse 17, **"IF** now I have found favor . . ." and even tells God, "Please do not depart from here until I come back to You" (v. 18). God reassures him again, "I will remain until you return." So Gideon does go with God and He tells him, "Peace to you, do not be afraid; you shall not die" (v. 23). Getting his mind straight, Gideon then "built an altar there to the LORD and named it The LORD is Peace" (v. 24). Oh that we would quit doubting with fears and let the God-factor take us to higher levels in life.

For now, we're going to rehearse many things God **DOES** which should raise your hope quotient. As you linger over the enormity of God's work for you, ask yourself if you believe this. Then remember, accept, and live like it's true. It'll make a difference in your thoughts, attitudes, choices, and actions.

God *Does* All of This for Us

Saves (Psm. 55:16; 138:7; 106:8, 10)

Protects (Psm. 121:7; 146:9)

Answers (Psm. 3:4; 99:6; 20:6)

Guards (Psm. 121:8; 127:1)

Restores (Ps. 85:1)

Delivers (Ps. 54:7)

Supplies (Phil. 4:19)

Understands (Psm. 33:15; 139:2)

Satisfies (Psm. 81:16; 103:5;)

Accepts (Rom. 14:3)

Knows (Psm. 44:21; 103:14)

Redeems (Psm. 49:15; 55:18; 103:4)

Gives (Psm. 29:11; 136:25;)

Will not abandon (Ps. 94:14)

Made me hope (Ps. 119:49)

Sustains (Psm. 3:5; 37:17; 55:22)

Hates injustice (Psm. 5:5; 45:7)

Hears (Psm. 4:3; 5:3; 28:6)

Shields (Ps. 59:11)

Heals (Psm. 103:3; 147:3)

Provides (Ps. 68:6)

Binds wounds (Ps. 147:3)

Keeps (Psm. 145:20; 121:7)

Lifts up (Ps. 30:1)

Sets me free (Rom. 8:2)

Renews (Ps. 104:30)

Binds us up (Isa. 61:1)

Watches over (Ps. 116:34)

Counsels (Ps. 32:8)

Fashioned me (Ps. 119:73)

Dwells in you (Rom. 8:9)

Intercedes (Rom. 8:26)

Delights (Isa. 62:4)

Thwarts wicked (Ps. 146:9)

Forgives (Ps. 78:38)

Loves (Prov. 3:12; John 3:16)

Rescues (Col. 1:13)

Guides (Psm. 73:24; 78:52)

Equips (2 Tim. 3:17)

Comforts (2 Cor. 1:3–7)

Supports fatherless (Ps. 146:9)

Helps weaknesses (Rom. 8:26)

Remembers (Ps. 111:5)

Leads us (2 Cor. 2:14)

Cares (1 Pet. 5:7)

Delivers (Psm. 34:19

Brought me up (Ps. 40:2)

Instructs (Psm 32:8)

Causes (Rom. 8:28)

Came to fulfill (Matt. 5:17)

Died (Rom. 6:10)

Was raised (Rom. 6:4)	**Loosed bonds** (Psm. 116:16)	**Grants** (1 Chron. 4:10)
Examines motives (Prov. 16:2)	**Is coming** (Ps. 98:9)	**Crowns** (Ps. 103:4)
Relieves me (Ps. 4:1)	**Created** (Ps. 89:47)	**Deals richly** (Psm. 142:7)
Establishes (Psm. 89:4; 103:19)	**Anointed** (2 Cor. 1:21)	**Never allows** (Psm. 55:22)
Called us (2 Tim. 1:9)	**Predestined us** (Rom. 8:30)	**Justified us** (Rom. 4:5)
Teaches (Psm. 71:17; 119:102)	**Endures** (Ps. 52:1)	**Favors the fearing** (Psm.2:7) **Sustains**
Reigns (Psm. 93:1; 99:1)	**Enlarges hearts** (Ps. 119:32)	**Clothes** (Ps. 132:16)
Made heaven & earth (Ps. 121:2)	**Rewards you** (Prov. 25:22)	**Founded earth** (Ps. 102:25)

When in doubt of all that God does for us, read the above list and, more importantly, read His Word. How could we possibly ever think He is not enough to meet our needs? We can always trust Him, and He will always work for our good. One of our pastors would say we need our heads examined from the hips both ways if we can't understand such deep truths.

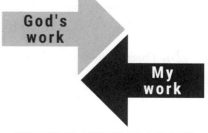

Unique combination of God's and man's work

God's work

My work

SPIRITUAL LIVING IN ACTION

Study Questions for Chapter 9: The God-Factor: The Bottom Line for All of Life

1. What steps are you motivated to take to allow the God-factor to be a high priority?

2. Daniel 11:32 reminds us of what?

3. What are the beginning pieces of a walk with God? See Romans 3:23; 5:8; 6:23; John 1:12; 3:16; 1 Corinthians 15:3–4; 1 John 1:9. It's who you know that gets you into _____. (Fill in the blank.)

4. List the various descriptions of God's character (**love** being sacrificial action to meet deep personal needs, **sovereign** being in control, etc.).

5. When are we made strong? See 2 Corinthians 12:9–10.

6. How do people act when they think they are their own god?

7. Do you really comprehend how big your God is? Read the lists aloud in this chapter, how God IS THE_____ and who HE IS. We must not forget these attributes.

8. Discuss what gets in our way to truly trust a big God, as presented in the many Scriptures in this chapter.

9. After reading all that God does for us, commit to spend regular time to look up all those verses for your personal pleasure. This will change your perspective about everything. Those who have chosen to allow the God-factor in their lives can live a very blessed life.

10. Discuss the sovereignty of God and the responsibility of man—how both are very important. It's the design of our heavenly Father. He didn't make us robots; we get choice and He does His work for us.

11. Share how God has made a difference in your life. (There are many listed in the chapter you can copy.)

10

Make Your Bible Come Alive
(Linda's Personal Bible Study Method)

We all know the Lord does not lead contrary to His Word. Our definitions of how life works need to come from Him. Second Samuel 22:29 says, "For you are my lamp, Lord: And the Lord illuminates my darkness." Making sure our Bible comes alive will neutralize cultural attempts to entice us to think and act differently. It gives us a moral and ethical compass to follow.

The reasons are numerous for why we need to make our Bible come alive. Psalm 16:7–8 gives us motivation: "I will bless the Lord who has advised me. Indeed, my mind instructs me in the night. I have set the Lord continually before me; Because He is at my right hand, I will not be shaken." You are developing a life protection system when you get to know your Bible.

We've spoken to the negative voices that influence us, yet it seems important to mention again some of the negative pulls that are increasingly strong. My sphere and I have noted an almost epidemic in (even Christian) young people refusing to honor their parents. Too many are deciding they no longer want anything to do with their parents and refuse to see or be involved with them, and without good reasons. Sometimes it's their friends who convince them of this, and unfortunately numbers are convincing their counselors that this is best for their future. The word *SAFE* has gone to seed, as many are running away from responsibility or God-ordered design because somehow, they have been convinced they are not "safe" in their present world. The culture is promoting fear factors about many things and then convincing even smart people they are not safe. Oh my. This is more than immaturity gone wild; it's godlessness.

This is why our making the Bible come alive is totally necessary, so we don't get distracted from the bottom line of what is designed and important.

Unless you are looking for certain things, it is easy to read right over the top of something and not notice what is there. The system below will help you **look** for specific essentials for spiritual living, **find,** and **mark** them with a color for easy locating.

The following analogy isn't in the same realm, but it makes a point. My husband used to be an archer. The rule was never aim to shoot your arrow at the whole target, but at a specific point. In our Bible study, we're going to be looking for specific spiritual truths. Stay with me.

If you don't have these specific truths close at hand in your mind, as you'll see below, you'll get into discouraging circumstances along the way in your life and be tempted to get overly depressed. You won't know how to handle hard situations and may run away in anger or disillusionment. You won't realize you have power and options. You will simply be off course. This process of making our Bible come alive gives us purpose, direction, and confidence to be all God intended.

For many years, I have been using this very simple system I developed to identify at a glance how my God has ordained life. I can flip through the pages of my Bible and quickly spot what He's like (in purple), what He has done and is doing for me (in blue), along with what my responsibilities (commands) are (in red), and the promises I can claim (in green). If I forget who I am as a converted child of God, I see at a glance (in yellow) what He has done for my eternal assurance and the difference that makes. There's more, but each aspect is identified by one of seven colors. My Bible has come alive with these markings. Below is the chart that shows what to look for.

Bible Study Method As Developed by Linda Weber

WHO GOD IS

(His character—surround each word describing
who God **is** in *purple*)

WHAT GOD DOES

(Action He takes—surround each word describing
what God **does** in *blue*)

COMMANDS/RESPONSIBILITIES

(The instructions in verbs where action is required—
surround each **command** in *red*)

PROMISES

(Arrow to the left if **promise** is positive, arrow to the right
for negative promises—in *green*)
Surround each **promise** phrase in green,
positive or consequences to expect

SALVATION TRUTHS

(Who and what we are now as believers,
what has happened—in *yellow*)
Surround words of the descriptions of our **salvation**
in yellow

EVALUATIONS

(Questions asked—surround questions asked in *orange*)
(This shows evaluations and questions being considered)

EXAMPLES

(To follow or avoid)
Surround the examples given in Scripture in *black*
for instant reference
(Arrows to the left of example for positive
and arrows to the right for negative to avoid)
(Arrows each way are in *black*)

Along with these seven categories, there are questions you can ask
yourself about each in the middle column. In the right-hand column
you will find action for you to take with each learned aspect.

The spiritual truth learned is	Answers to my questions	Action to commit to
	Am I realizing what all of this means when I learn these new truths that need response?	
Who God IS	What He is to me	**Develop** an educated awareness of Him.
		Remember it, **meditate** on it, have something to **fix on**.
		Place this knowledge in my mental reservoir.
		Follow and **mirror** this model.
		Let light shine out any darkness and **fill** my life.
What God DOES	What He has done for me	**Remember**, lest I forget; **be prepared to speak of it.**
	What He is doing for me	**Ponder** implication.
	What He will do for me	**Live** like it's true; **Pattern** my life after His example (there is a lot to work on).
		Celebrate His faithfulness. **Thank** Him for the blessings and **help** through it all.
Commands/ Responsibilities	What expectations He makes of me	**Observe, do, keep,** and **act upon** them.
		Obey, take personal responsibility.
		Evaluate my choice.
		Determine to follow the godly way.
		Talk to the Lord about these.
		Ask God to show me more ways **to follow** Him.
		Make myself **accountable** so as not to be avoiding visible commands.

The spiritual truth learned is	Answers to my questions	Action to commit to
Commands/ Responsibilities (continued)	What expectations He makes of me	**Identify** my personal profile to assure keeping the commands. Identify how I must make it practical action in my life.
Promises	What promises He has given me to claim.	**Claim** and **believe** them.
		Learn to understand them. **Dissolve** any unbelief with this truth.
		Choose to walk away from nagging wrong fears of whatever feeds insecurity.
Salvation Truths	What we were and are now after becoming God's child.	**Know and enjoy** my new position in Christ after accepting Him.
		Tell others. **Give thanks** repeatedly for this reality.
	What the requirements are for salvation.	**Live like you are heaven bound.**
		Let your light **shine.** **Take pleasure** knowing the process.
Evaluations	What are these questions about?	**Be** introspective for understanding.
		Pay attention to what is happening.
Examples	What others have done for our instruction	**Learn** from them, and **act** accordingly.
		Repeat the positive, and **avoid** the negatives and potholes.

You are familiarizing yourself with what God is like (do remember the Holy Spirit is the power behind everything) and then, what He expects of you—wonderful. Those two doctrines of the sovereignty of God and the responsibility of man are all continually spelled out in Scripture. Both are true.

As you mark your Bible with these seven colors—identifying at a glance how God is fighting for you, how He's promised you the world, and is big enough to handle anything you ever have to deal with—you are going to experience life in a more productive and powerful way. "The Word of God is living and active and sharper than any two-edged sword, even penetrating as far as the division of soul and spirit, of both joints and marrow, and able to judge the thoughts and intentions of the heart" (Heb. 4:12).

Study Questions for Chapter 10: Make Your Bible Come Alive (Linda's Personal Bible Study Method)

1. Do you need some light to shine in any areas of darkness of your life? See 2 Samuel 22:29 and tell how it can happen.

2. Do you ever wish you could get answers in the night as your mind is weighed down over issues? See Psalm 16:7–8 and tell how this can happen.

3. If you need life protection systems, share how you can get it. See Psalm 118:8–9.

4. Do you wish you could get your Bible to come alive so you don't get so distracted, wondering how to find anything relevant? What has been your method to find God's design for you?

5. List the seven categories Linda suggests you look for and highlight them. What are the colors for each as you make each aspect stand out in your Bible? (You are going to be amazed how you will have the facts so organized! As you thumb through your Bible, it will make so much sense to quickly find these gems so you can take action.)

6. List the action verbs in the chapter describing what to do with each of the seven discoveries. Review this in the text. There is a long list of responsibilities for us to grasp.

7. With all these specific discoveries in your Bible reading, are you predicting the lights to be coming on for you to have the mind of the Lord to fill your mental file drawers? There is nothing more beautiful.

8. Read Hebrews 4:12 again and spend some time appreciating the fact the Word of God is "living and active, and sharper than any two-edged sword, even penetrating as far as the division of soul and spirit, of both joints and marrow, and able to judge the thoughts and intentions of the heart."

9. As you look at John 8:32, you will relax in the fact when you know the truth, it will make you _____. (Fill in the blank.) Then read John 8:36.

10. Discuss how your views can change as you find morsels to see life through God's glasses. Discuss your anticipation to know better how to view life not through circumstances, your difficult childhood, your experiences, or your need to control, but as God gives you awareness of His character. Review who God is, what He does, the commands He gives us, the promises we have to count on, the examples He graciously provides, and more. It changes our lives— do you see it coming?

Overcoming to Thrive with Jesus: How and What

B ottom line: you were never intended to handle the hundreds of hardships people face every day by yourself. We have a big God and He expects you to come to Him with your burdens. First Peter 5:7 tells us, "Cast all your anxiety on Him, because He cares about you." Don't set yourself for disappointment in trying to do things by yourself—you have Jesus. Besides, He gives us other likeminded Christian friends to share our load. Philippians 2:25 helps us see how these brothers needed Epaphroditus, a fellow worker and soldier, to help meet needs together. Don't try proceeding alone.

We were designed to be overcomers—to be and do together, not alone. Our God is a picture of togetherness in the person of the Trinity—Father, Son, and Spirit, being one. God didn't want Adam to be alone; He created a helpmate. Ecclesiastes 4:12 says, "A cord of three strands is not quickly torn apart." Jesus provides physical means for us to accomplish being overcomers. Even the US Army expects their soldiers to stick together. My husband reflects often on his Ranger/battle buddy who they assign to protect, support, and do everything together. The Scripture is full of "one anothering" commands, telling us to be stronger people as we do things with and for others. We need people around us to help keep us straight.

This overcoming concept is seen in numerous realms. "In a horse-pulling contest at a county fair, the first-place horse moved a sled weighing 4,500 pounds. The runner-up had pulled 4,000 pounds. The owners of the two horses wondered how much the animals could pull if they worked together. So they hitched them up and loaded the sled. To everyone's surprise, the horses were able to pull 12,000 pounds."[1] Together is better.

We share our issues with people of like mind to find encouragement and direction as we guide each other. It's a powerful force. When prisons want to take power away from a prisoner, the inmate is placed in solitary confinement because isolation stops and prevents strength in numbers.

I've gone through the material of this book with many people, and the response is heartwarming. I wouldn't have guessed a doctoral college professor would say the big thing she returns to is the graphic below. This is the real power behind overcoming. It's a lady plugging her washing machine into the electric socket, the power source, so it will function. The point being, we must access our power source to accomplish our missions in life. You are then empowered beyond anything you can do on your own.

You must access the power source

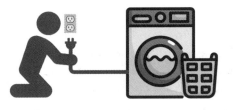

There's power in prayer—may we never forget this. Corrie ten Boom said, "The wonderful thing about praying is that you leave a world of not being able to do something, and enter God's realm where everything is possible."[2] Corrie spent her life helping people know they must be filled with the Holy Spirit. She'd tell people there is no optional command in the Bible—it was absolutely necessary. She'd refer to the earthly disciples and how they could have never stood up under the persecution of the Jews and Romans had they not waited for Pentecost. She reminded everybody that each of us needs our own personal Pentecost, the baptism of the Holy Spirit. Her directive to all is we will never be able to stand in the tribulation without it.

Corrie had to endure unspeakable conditions in the horrible Nazi concentration camp. Her response? "When I am weak, then I shall be strong, the Bible says." As a prisoner she got power because the Holy Spirit was upon her. The mighty inner strengthening of the Holy Spirit helped her through. She said, "No, you will not be strong in yourself when the tribulation comes. Rather, you will be strong in the power of Him who will not forsake you. For seventy-six years I have known the Lord Jesus and not once has He ever left me or let me down." She goes on to quote Job 13:15, "'Though He slay me, yet will I trust Him,' for I know that to all who overcome, He shall give the crown of life. Hallelujah!"[3]

It is wonderful when we can find real-life illustrations of how the power we need to overcome happens not from ourselves but from above. "Eagle does not fight the snake on the ground. It picks it up into the sky and changes the battle ground, and then it releases the snake into the sky. The snake has no stamina, no power and no balance in the air."[4] This becomes very obvious of how we must take our fight into the spiritual realm by praying. When we are in the spiritual realm, God takes over our battles. Don't fight the enemy in his comfort zone—change the battle ground like the eagle and let God take charge through our earnest prayer.

We like to think we can do it all and we do try, but when we access the power of God, we are not on our own. I have a beautifully crafted treatment of Scripture over our TV reminding us where our power is. Isaiah 40:31 says, "Those who **wait** for the LORD Will gain new strength; They will mount up with wings like eagles, They will run and not get tired, They will walk and not become weary." I love that.

Whether it's little things or big things, we can tap into the power of our God to accomplish our missions in life. We can overcome. God raised Lazarus from the dead. He's made blind men see. He's given babies to women past their fertile years. He parted the Red Sea for Moses to go through on dry land. He closed the lions' mouths for Daniel's safety. He can accomplish whatever He deems right.

You may be guilty of verbalizing that God can't do this or that. You might say, "I've just had too many bad things to live through to actually make it." Consider this comment, "Your journey will be much lighter and easier if you don't carry your past with you."[5] What things in life could be causing you to be "hung up"?

We each have a different package of things to deal with in life. The intensity and depth of the issues are all over the map. This story I'm about to share with you could not have happened if it weren't for the incredible power of God to change a life. Whatever our lot, God's grace is greater. The following is a quote from this man in his own words:

4 felonies, 8 misdemeanors, 2 hit and runs, 4 DUI's, 5 car wrecks, broke into churches at 2 am in the morning high off pills. Was sent to prison at 17. Lost 2 brothers one murdered and one who passed away in a car wreck late at night, lived with a foster family I never heard of before, didn't go to college, didn't have a dad around to show me how to do this thing called life, all I had was an amazing mother who did her best and my decisions.

And somewhere along the road Grace showed up and changed my whole world. I'm engaged to a beautiful woman who loves Jesus. I'm going on my 3rd year as a business owner. I've been a youth pastor here in SC for over 15 months and God has given me the opportunity to speak and share my story with 100s of people.

Life isn't fair. This is a fact. I was 17 years old headed to prison because of my stupid decisions. 22 years old addicted to alcohol and Xanax bars because I let the enemy trick me and now here I was in a rehab wondering what it is I'm going to do with my life when I get out. Then Jesus showed up. I said yes to the offer He gave me and I've never went back since.

Quit playing with life. Living for the pleasures of now and forsaking your God given destiny. Jesus is the way, the truth and the life.

By yourself it's pointless, but if you give it over to Him, you will have peace that's unspeakable and joy that's uncontainable. Don't fight on your own. There is a God above who loves and wants you but he will not force his way into your life. You'll have to make decision just like I did and run after Him with everything inside of you.[6]

Oh my goodness. That says it big time. Only the power of God could have drawn him out of all that and turned him around marvelously.

I have a file of many people who have had a mindset to overcome. There is the story of a teen who spent his free time setting track records. He literally runs on two prosthetic legs and sets world junior amputee sprint records.[7]

Another is a teen who battled disease. Katie never saw herself as being disabled and she had a tremendous optimistic attitude. "I know better what it really means to try to make a difference when the stakes are life itself. If you live in the valley of the shadow of death, you realize which peaks are really worth climbing." She goes on to say, "Positive thinking is the best way to get through bad times."[8]

We all need the power of peace in our lives. Philippians 4:7 says, "And the peace of God, which surpasses all comprehension, will guard your hearts and your minds in Christ Jesus." He goes on to help us get it. Verses 8–9 say, "Finally, brothers and sisters, whatever is true, whatever is honorable, whatever is right, whatever is pure, whatever is lovely, whatever is commendable, if there is any excellence and if anything worthy of praise, think about these things. As for the things you have learned and received and heard and seen in me, practice these things, and the God of peace will be with you."

My good friends, Al and Lisa Robertson from the *Duck Dynasty* family, point to my favorite verse, Luke 1:37: "Nothing will be impossible with God" as they share how their past doesn't have to determine their future. They tell their story of broken vows and ultimate redemption in their book, *A New Season*. There was infidelity, deceit, distrust, and shame. They show how they learned to rebuild lost love and rebuild trust. They would say their hope can become anyone's hope, and restoration can take place in any marriage. Their pain-filled honesty can encourage you to overcome your own personal story of pain to experience redemption in your home.

Dave Dravecky played for the San Francisco Giants MLB team for three years but ended up losing an arm. During his hospital times he found people who were going through very hard things. One lady who was riddled with cancer shared about her faith with him; he felt she had more pearls of wisdom than he could come close to. She told Dave that every morning she would look at a picture of Jesus at the foot of her bed, saying He's "the author and perfecter of faith" (Heb. 12:2). With what Jesus went through she felt she could endure the cancer for another day. This woman taught him to see Jesus again. There's power there.[9]

On one hand you may know **about** God's power and the blessings we possess with Him. You may know all the right ways to go. Then, some will take it further and **access** this wonderful power. (How badly do we want to see things really happen?) But, there's the other side of our head that might refute it all and whisper to our mind, *No, you don't have to make all those God-like choices. You have rights and need to do what feels best for you. After all, you are important. Do what you want to do. You don't need God; you're great on your own.*

Scripture speaks to everything. Bottom line is this: Matthew 6:24 says, "No one can serve two masters; for either he will hate the one and love the other, or he will be devoted to one and despise the other. You cannot serve God and wealth." We try to entertain opposite sides of what is best but it doesn't work.

Are we guilty of dividing our minds? Philippians 4:6 tells us, "Do not be anxious about anything, but in everything by prayer and pleading with thanksgiving let your requests be made known to God." I've heard my husband preach for years now, and that verse in the original language means to stop dividing your mind. That rings a little clearer to us than not being anxious. Our new nature does battle with our old nature and they both have different directions they are leading us. Let's listen to those right God messages and follow His leading as opposed to what will take us astray. This is the secret to overcoming.

Our mindset helps us through the small, lesser things in life too. My city league tennis partner and I had just lost a first set 1–6 in our match. I told her I have been behind 0–5 before and came back to win a set 7–5. I shared how I'm writing this book on mindset and we can get our

Stop dividing your mind

God knows my circumstances...

I am important...

I am thankful...

I have a right to be down...

God doesn't care...

I am complete in God...

Nobody likes me...

I have security in Jesus...

I'll never make it...

I'm confident...

Injustice is all I face...

mindset in gear here and do this. We *knew* we could play better than we just had shown. We won the next set 7–5 which took us to the tie breaker. The mindset kicked in and we won the tie breaker against this youthful, wealthy club team, 10–6. We all must apply our wills to a strong mindset as we go up against everything. This changes things.

Like anything in life, to get the product (overcoming to thrive with Jesus), there needs to be a process beforehand. And, like we have told our kids over the years, with privilege comes responsibility. We naturally want the privileges but not so much the preceding work. We're going to look at more Scriptures that spell out both privileges and the responsibilities we must meet prior to the privileges. This again will help us grasp the need to do our part in order to overcome our various difficulties.

Privilege		*Responsibility*
Psalm 146:5	Blessed is he	**whose help** is the God of Jacob, **whose hope** is in the LORD his God
Psalm 145:14	The LORD supports all who fall and raises up	all who **are bowed down**
Psalm 145:18–19	The LORD is near to all	who **call** upon Him
	He will fulfill the desire of those He will also hear their cry for help and will save them.	who **fear** Him
Psalm 145:20	The LORD watches over all	who **love** Him
1 John 5:14	He hears us	if we **ask** anything **according to His will**
Psalm 37:4	He will give you the desires of your heart	**Delight** yourself in the LORD
Psalm 119:165	You will have great peace, and nothing causes them to stumble	Those who **love** Your law
Proverbs 2:7	He stores up sound wisdom He is a shield	for the **upright**; to those who **walk in integrity**
Proverbs 5:1–2	So that you may maintain discretion and your lips may comply with knowledge	**Pay attention** to my wisdom **Incline** your ear to my understanding
Proverbs 4:5–9	And she will guard you	**Acquire** wisdom! **Acquire** understanding! **Do not forget nor turn away** from the words of my mouth. **Do not abandon** her.
	She will watch over you and she will exalt you	**Love** her, **Acquire** wisdom; and with all your possessions, **acquire** understanding

Proverbs 4:5–9 (continued)	She will exalt you	**Prize** her
	She will honor you	if you **embrace** her
	She will place on your head a garland of grace; she will present you with a crown of beauty	
Proverbs 4:10	The years of your life will be many	**Accept** my sayings
Psalm 133:1	How good and how pleasant it is	For brothers to **live together in unity**
Psalm 55:22	He will sustain you; He will never allow the righteous to be shaken	**Cast** your burden upon the LORD

Overcoming will happen when you have a directed life. What more can He do but keep promising us the world—let's listen, believe, and thrive through it all. Every day is an opportunity to exceed your personal limits. Review a few promises from God's Word; they will leave you with overwhelming confidence.

- "We may receive mercy and find grace for help at the time of our need" (Heb. 4:16).
- "I can do all things through Him who strengthens me" (Phil. 4:13).
- "I am confident . . . that He who began a good work among you will complete it by the day of Christ Jesus" (Phil 1:6).
- "Through Him we both have our access in one Spirit to the Father" (Eph 2:18).
- "God has not given us a spirit of timidity, but of power and love and discipline" (2 Tim. 1:7).
- "We have boldness and confident access through faith in Him" (Eph. 3:12).
- "Who will separate us from the love of Christ? Will tribulation, or trouble, or persecution, or famine, or nakedness, or danger, or sword?" (Rom. 8:35).

"Strength doesn't come from what you can do. Strength comes from overcoming the things you thought you couldn't."[10] And, that's the work of the living God in you to make that happen, as you LET Him. For success, jump over those hurdles like the track winner does in his race, not just questioning why they are there.

Overcoming for success is the combination of God's powerful sovereignty in our lives and personal responsibility. It means obeying God and doing our own due diligence with many factors: working hard, facing rejections with God's skills, making sacrifices, showing discipline, handling criticism artfully, willing to take risks, and facing losses with God's help. Everybody has some sort of challenging and troublesome situation in their lives. "Things" aren't working out like we could have wished. As a matter of fact, "things" need a lot of adjusting. We need to do a lot of diverting so we don't go down with the ship.

When things are weighing you down severely, your mindset determines your health and well-being. We do our best to rectify hard things but then we have to let go and watch how God will work the rest of our tapestry. Because there is obvious evil in our world, we have the personal opportunity to refuse surrendering to such dark ways by assuring our mindset is set to remember that God is greater.

We must divert

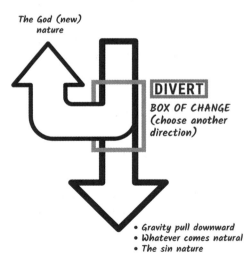

The God (new) nature

DIVERT
BOX OF CHANGE
(choose another direction)

• Gravity pull downward
• Whatever comes natural
• The sin nature

I know everybody has a list of negatives in their lives and the intensity of these are all very different. We're going to work together on how to process these issues. Your mental toughness will be necessary and not allowing yourselves to dwell on what seems to be impossible. We're going to break the chain of defeat. So, like with anything electronic, you need to REBOOT, and then divert.

DIVERT—This is a strong factor needed in our process of overcoming in life. Do you remember that arrow pointing downward which we've already discussed? We're born with this natural gravity-like force taking us down, to live for self. It's the sin nature. We need to turn the wheel and DIVERT to get off a wayward doomed track. It will involve removing ourselves from the pull taking us away, otherwise we are literally hung up and not free to enjoy the godly intention.

Matthew 6:24 says, "No one can serve two masters; for either he will hate the one and love the other, or he will be devoted to one and despise the other."

The dictionary definition of *divert* means, "to turn aside or from a path or course; deflect. To draw to a different course or purpose."[11] This definition carries a very serious concept for us to incorporate.

Getting off a "pre-decided" path requires who you know. Knowing God enables you a power that is above all. (It's who you know that gets you into heaven.) And it's that same "who you know" and "box of change" who takes you in a different direction. DIVERTING off that original destination of an eternity without God to a new direction toward heaven, with new spiritual goals in life. Your God-shaped vacuum has been filled with the living God. Old things have become new (2 Cor. 5:17).

DIVERTING will display the new person, as you choose to obey God's intentions. (Disobedience has its separate consequences.) What is affected? Everything—how you prioritize everything, who you listen to, who you please, how you make decisions, what you give yourself to, who you run with, why you do what you do, how you make goals, how you spend your time and money, how you raise your family, what habits you allow, and more.

We must forever remember we cannot control other people's responses to anything. We are responsible for our own responses and that is where your power is. Turning the wheel and going that different direction first of all gives us new life in Christ. We are recalculating our path (a familiar process we do in our travels with the GPS). We are resetting our minds. All those choices of how we live are facing us. We shake the dust off and go a different way. When diverting, let's consider some new patterns:

- Visualize positive potential and good, rather than capitalizing on negative restrictions
- Ask God how He would choose for me to proceed
- Choose thankfulness rather than discontentedness and complaining; find the blessings
- Persevere rather than give up with hopelessness; try again when something doesn't work
- Ask myself if my habits are pleasing to God
- Pursue God's desires for me as written in His Word; train my mind with His ways
- Display the fruit of the Spirit as opposed to negative behaviors
- Avoid temptations to displease God; refuse evil and destruction
- Think big and with a positive mindset to overcome; bask in God's goodness
- Choose honesty; speak truth
- Do unto others as I'd have them do unto me; overcome evil with good
- Place your hang ups on the cross and learn the better way
- Live my life in a way that people see Jesus in me
- Consider how Scripture says there is wisdom/victory in an abundance of (good) counselors (Prov. 11:14)
- Be involved with healthy God-honoring people, listening to the right voices
- Choose the high road and not "getting in the mud" with troubled people
- Forgive like Jesus does so I am not held hostage by my stubbornness
- Disallow resentment and bitterness to enjoy a healthy life, and honor God, regardless circumstances
- Not fearing everything around the corner, being skeptical
- Rehearsing God's character, promises and expectations
- Choose to trust my trustworthy God
- Get honest with my sin so as not to be trapped in an unhappy life; be free indeed
- Erase the fog on my windshields of God's understanding by reading the Bible

- Look beyond the trials to the blue sky of how God will use all for my good
- Determine to keep going up the "down staircase" in life

I hope the word *divert* will become an action word you incorporate into your everyday world. There are too many issues to distract us from being who God created us to be. One of our friends adopted a troubled youth who was continually doing things his own way and making bad decisions. Bless our friend's response. He took this young man up close to his face and called him by name quietly saying, "There is a better way." In other words, divert from the wrong way. May we choose **the better way** instead of going in all directions in a frenzy. Meditating on the better way will set us up for success when the trouble sets in.

It's so typical for us to proceed with what has been "normal" or "standard" in our home of origin or later. It's the pattern we know so we keep doing it—it's familiar. Unfortunately, we keep going down the dark alleys and getting mugged instead of making a change. We repeat chaotic patterns, setting ourselves up for more of the same. Remaining in a traumatic status does not win friends and influence people, nor does it help those closest to us. Insane, wouldn't you say? We can DIVERT! That is the way God can take you through your wildernesses. You must see yourself accurately to proceed in the better way.

We need practical suggestions to determine how to do all this. We can't allow overspending, overeating, overdrinking, overreacting, over-committing to an unreasonable amount of responsibilities. We say no to dangerous activities. Of course, anything illegal only complicates everything. You probably need a wise friend to walk beside you and coach you in keeping you on the straight and narrow, especially if you have a history of getting away from the straight line.

So much starts in our brains. Proverbs 23:7 says, "As he thinks within himself, so he is." Are you programmed in your brain to soar or fail? Are you programmed to win or lose? Are you programmed to trust or fear? Are you programmed to feel blessings or burdens? Are you predictable with either of these tendencies? Do you find a way to make good things happen, or do you insist nothing will ever work, maybe catastrophizing? You get the privilege of making the choice of going one way or the other. You rewrite the script. Let's get out of failure mode into the mind of Christ.

A question to ask ourselves would be, what do I fix my mind on? Trouble or blessing? If it's sinful pleasures, a dominating status, or a greedy heart, we're in trouble. Is it loose friends? You can name your own weaknesses. I don't want you swimming in a sea of sharks. So let's look at more Scripture in light of your learning to divert to overcome in life, to thrive with Jesus. "Do the Bible" as one of our church leaders has said.

- "Let's **rid ourselves** of every obstacle and the sin which so easily entangles us, and **let's run** with endurance the race that is set before us, **looking only at** Jesus, the originator and perfecter of the faith, who for the joy set before Him endured the cross" (Heb. 12:1–2).
- "**Clean out** the old leaven so that you may be a new lump, just as you are in fact unleavened" (1 Cor. 5:7).
- "**Repent** and **return**, so that your sins may be wiped away, in order that times of refreshing may come from the presence of the Lord" (Acts 3:19).
- "**Let love be without hypocrisy. Detest** what is evil; cling to what is good" (Rom. 12:9).
- "**Keep away** from every brother or sister who leads a disorderly life and not one in accordance with the tradition which you received from us" (2 Thess. 3:6).
- "**Do not participate** in the useless deeds of darkness, but instead even **expose** them" (Eph. 5:11).
- "**Rid yourselves of** all of them: anger, wrath, malice, slander, and obscene speech from your mouth. **Do not lie** to one another, since you stripped off the old self with its evil practices and have **put on** the new self who is being renewed to a true knowledge according to the image of the One who created it" (Col. 3:8–10).
- "**See that no one deceive** you with empty words; for because of these things the wrath of God comes upon the sons of

disobedience. Therefore **do not become partners** with them" (Eph. 5:6–7).

Consider the words of Booker T. Washington, "Success is to be measured not so much by the position one has reached in life as by the obstacles which he has overcome while trying to succeed."[12] You will have obstacles, and you can overcome them. God gives you power; you determine to do your part.

Study Questions for Chapter 11: Overcoming to Thrive with Jesus: How and What

1. What factors have you learned that display how we should not remain alone in our life quest?

2. Despite your difficult circumstances, is it possible to overcome? Memorize Matthew 19:26.

3. What is the source of real power to overcome? See Acts 1:8; Proverbs 8:17.

4. If you are waiting on the Lord, whose strength are you plugging into? See Isaiah 40:13.

5. Do we understand how powerful our minds are when we allow a state of anxiety to prevail? Discuss the meaning of anxiety (stop dividing your mind—Phil. 4:6) and tell how we get into trouble with this.

6. When you are overcoming, you are meeting the many admonitions in Scripture. Name some Scripture that shows the privileges you get when meeting the active responsibilities given.

7. Because the sin nature is like gravity, what one word from the text reminds you of action you must take to stop the natural bend? See Matthew 6:24; Romans 12:2.

8. On what do you fix your mind? Write out the verbs in the following verses that display the needed action on your part: Hebrews

12:1; Acts 3:19; Romans 12:9; 2 Thessalonians 3:6. There are more listed in the chapter text for your "extra credit."

Security in Life Comes from Being God-Centered

One of my grandsons had a shirt he loved to wear pretty much all the time. His brother who is more clothes-conscious would ask his bro why he needs to wear that shirt all the time. The answer was easy, *I like it*. He didn't care what everybody else thought about what he wore because he liked it. He felt secure and didn't have anything to prove. It's refreshing to observe folks who know who they are and who don't try to be something or someone they are not.

How many of us feel very comfortable wearing clothes others may think aren't expensive enough, or aren't of the latest style? In high school I could have wished I had some nice clothes. We didn't happen to have anybody who gave us hand-me-downs either, but we lived in our mom's wake that this wasn't a focus in life. It was okay. Nobody measured our friendship on clothes or cars. The other kids liked us regardless the material things. I was lucky enough to be able to get to high school in a car, albeit a very laughable kind of car. It was transportation. I certainly couldn't take my confidence from that car, but I didn't think about it (much).

Different things make us feel secure or important. What school did you go to and what kind of pay do you enjoy from your job? How nice a house do you live in and would people have a good enough time coming to your less-than-terrific house? Can you serve exotic foods to make everybody have a fun time at your place? Maybe it's the vacation options you have. Do you go to far-away hot spots everybody loves to talk about? Can you afford all the things those around you are bragging about? What is it that makes you feel secure?

One very wealthy man was asked how much money was enough. His quick answer: "Just a little bit more." It doesn't matter what level you're at, that answer would fit so many people. Having more money makes them feel secure.

Being in charge, making other people do what you want can make one feel secure. Watching people change at your command gives that feeling of power. They think intimidating others gives them security. We see it on the road all the time, where some drivers think they are more important than the next person, forcing others to move over, or not letting them in. They can feel so much better when they speed by you to show how big they are.

In the sporting world, there's power in the umpire/referee world, where their calls can turn a game one way or another. I know of one comment from a professional who actually said they are paid to make the game interesting, not necessarily fair. They feel so secure when they get to decide how things turn out. We can always hope for a fair official calling the shots for our desired team.

How about physical beauty? We are all endowed differently. It's the smart thing to make the most of what you've been given. The Creator designed us all differently, so can we accept His design? Do I choose to be happy with what He has made? (Go to Psalm 139 and enjoy the extensive pleasure of God forming your every part.) There are many Scriptures to remind us of all that. Isaiah 46:4 says, "Even to your old age I will be the same, And even to your graying years I will carry you! I have done it, and I will bear you; And I will carry you and I will save you."

To what extent do we think we need to enhance what He's given us? Can we feel secure in who we are or do we have to make changes? What drives us to be obsessed with our bodies? How much is too much? Personally, I like to do makeup even on days I'm not going anywhere or being with others. However, overdoing anything is always a consideration to be weighed—I don't want to be obsessive about it.

The subject of weight is a battle for many. Taking good care of our health is totally smart and responsible. Feeling secure can come when you do your honest best. Yet it's a trap if we take it to a different level, replacing the spiritual with the physical. Do we obsess on youthfulness as opposed to the authenticity of quality aging? Do we take our position on body aging from the media and the culture around us to feel good about ourselves? Feeling secure about who we are in our heart keeps us from getting disoriented. May we never exchange the truth of God's declarations for the worship of the culture's gods—body first in all its lures.

I admit, the Bible does mention gray hair in a positive light. Proverbs 20:29 says, "the honor of old men is their gray hair." I admit, I would be gray if I didn't color my hair, and yet I don't plan on letting gray be my color. So am I going against an honor code here not letting gray hair rule? I'm feeling secure without placing my value on how I'm received.

Security is an internal quality and much needed as a foundation on which to build. If there are cracks in the base, with improper reinforcements, things are going to crumble. As in buildings, there must be ethical engineering, adhering to safety standards, honoring building codes and more. If the load-bearing walls have flaws, there will be crumbling. If maintenance has been overlooked, the security is at stake. Construction of the basics will ensure the prevention of disasters downline.

If you study the ten worst high-rise building collapses in history, you see these principles violated in the demise of these huge structures with much tragedy. Security at the base is essential for longevity. Some work had been done illegally. You cannot eliminate support columns. Shortcuts financially cause destruction later. Overloaded materials cause disasters. The consequences of not dealing with the basics at first bring on predictable bad results. Lives are lost.[1]

The transfer of concepts from buildings to human psyches to be secure is rather obvious. As you ponder these realities, you will grasp the enormity of developing our secure mental, psychological, and spiritual base. Being a secure person doesn't just happen.

A parent's influence in raising a child is so important beyond the physical realm. We must go below the surface. Yes, the mental development is important, helping them learn the basics, getting them good schooling and their minds well trained. But below that level is the psychological level where their feelings are developed. If we don't take time to realize the ramifications here, we pay large prices along the way. And, then at the root, is the spiritual development where the heart is secure. This subject is vast needing us to take life to levels that will produce beautiful security with lived-out blessings. If we don't steer our kids within the spiritual realm, they will get steered by other forces lurking closely. Stay very involved with your kids' world, working way beyond the surface.

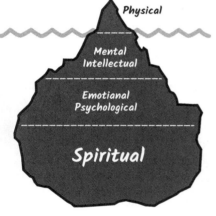

Security happens in the spiritual realm

Physical

Mental Intellectual

Emotianal Psychological

Spiritual

When you are a secure person, it's not going to bother you when you don't win a Grammy. It won't bother you if you haven't traveled the world. It won't bother you that you don't have the perfect body. When you make a mistake, it'll be okay as it's not the end of the world. Everybody makes mistakes. Your cooking or your speaking abilities are not to be compared to anybody because you are you, created uniquely by the Almighty God. So, who are you? (Consider listening to a song sung by Jessica Andrews called "Who I Am" to speak to this concept.)[2]

When you have become a child of God, by your active choice, you can relax knowing you are totally accepted. John 1:12, "As many as received Him, to them He gave the right to become children of God, to those who believe in His name." You are now born of God—that is foundational. Colossians 2:10 goes on, "In Him you have been made complete, and He is the head over all rule and authority."

There's no end in how I'm seen by my Creator. John 15:16 reminds us, "You did not choose Me but I chose you, and appointed you that you would go and bear fruit, and that your fruit would remain, so that whatever you ask of the Father in my name He may give to you." I am significant to Him! If we're not feeling secure, it's because we're not listening to Him who says different. We've been pronounced forever free from condemnation. Romans 8:1–2, convinces, "Therefore there is now no condemnation **at all** for those who are in Christ Jesus. For the law of the Spirit of life in Christ Jesus has set you free from the law of sin and of death."

I feel sorry for the folks who can't get this message through to their brain. God can handle whatever I face. I am His and He cares. He fights for me. His grace is sufficient, so why do I consider thinking differently? He is enough. He is able and I am not on my own. His powers can override the fear knocking on my door regularly. I can be still and know He is God and right beside me all the way. He has overcome the world, and I can overcome Satan's whispered temptations. I am secure in Him.

I hope you will take time to study this presentation of what security looks like in the God-centered person. Put yourself next to these descriptions from Scripture and ask yourself how you're doing. So often, the best of people do not see themselves. To live out this profile, it takes constant choice as to whether it is important to live up to a God-honoring standard. We have the power. We have the promises. We are able if we will just choose to live this way. Remember, it's turning the wheel on that downhill trek of gravity to enjoy this better way. God be with you as you go in the right direction.

Being God-centered displays security
(a well-founded confidence)

BEING WISE
Matthew 7:24 "hear & act ...a wise person"
- Accurate Assessment of Self (not too high, not too low)

James 3:17
- Wisdom from above is first:
  - Pure
  - Peaceable
  - Gentle
  - Reasonable
  - Full of Mercy
  - Good Fruits
  - Unwavering
  - Without Hypocrisy

BEING FULL OF HOPE
Psalms 46
- God is my refuge and strength

James 3:13
Who among you is wise and understanding? Let him show by his good behavior his deeds in the gentleness of wisdom.

ENDURING HARDSHIP
- Discern
- *Galatians 6* - Persevere Don't lose heart in doing good, for in due time ...

DISPLAYING OPTIMISM
Philippians 4:8
- Dwelling on whatever is:
  - True
  - Honorable
  - Right
  - Pure
  - Lovely
  - Of Good Repute
  - Any excellence
  - Anything worthy of praise

DISPLAYING FRUIT OF THE SPIRIT -
Galatians 5:22
- Love
- Joy
- Peace
- Patience
- Kindness
- Goodness
- Faithfulness
- Gentleness
- Self Control (forebearance)

Matthew 7:16
You will know them by their fruit.

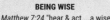

SUPERNATURAL
GOD CENTERED
REFLECTIONS
SECURITY

REFLECTING REST, PEACE, AND CONTENTMENT
- Contrite Spirit
- Settled
- Abandonment to God (end to self & having to be right)
- *Psalms 46* Cease striving and know the I am God
- *James 3:18* The seed whose fruit is righteousness is sown in peace by those who make peace.

REFLECTING GOD'S HEART
- Honesty
- Humility
- Compassion
- Mercy
- Balance
- *Ephesians 5:1* - Imitators of God
- Righteous
- *James 3:18* - The seed whose fruit is righteousness is sown in peace by those who make peace.

UNDERSTANDING AND SUBMITING TO:
- **Authority** - Romans 13:1 There is no authority except from God.
- **Boundaries** - Philippians 4:8 "whatever is true, honorable, right, pure,
- **God's way is best** - Hosea 14:9 The ways of the Lord are right

BEING OTHERS ORIENTED
Galatians
- Serve one another (5:13)
- Love neighbor as self (5:14)
- Bear one another's burdens and thus fulfill the law of Christ. If anyone thinks he is something when is nothing, he deceives himself. (6:2-3)
- Whatever you want others to do for you, do so for them (Matthew 7:12)

FOCUSING ON A BIG GOD
- He knows it all & beforehand (Nothing takes Him by surprise):
- He is **OMNISCIENT**
- In control of it all: **SOVEREIGN**
- Able to handle all I face: **OMNIPOTENT**
- Dispels confusion: **ALL WISE**
- Always fair: **JUST**
- His way is perfect: **GOOD**
- Never makes mistakes: **IMMUTABLE**
- Always keeps His promises: **FAITHFUL**
- Never leaves me: **OMNIPRESENT**
- Sacrificed to meet my needs: **LOVE**

WALKING WORTHY OF GOD'S CALLING
Ephesians 4 & 5
- Putting on the new self (in the likeness of God)
- Laying aside falsehood, speaking truth
- No longer darkened in one's understanding; all things become visible
- *1 Peter 1:13* - Gird your minds for action
- *Ephesians 5:1* - Pursue godliness imitate God
- *Matthew 6:33* - Seek first His Kingdom

SAYING "NO" TO ...
- *Colossians 3:9* the old self
- *Ephesians 4:25* - Lay aside falsehood (1/2 truths)
- *Ephesians 5:3* - Do not let ... impurity, greed
- *Galatians 6:7* - Do not be deceived
- *Ephesians 4:29* - Let no unwholesome word proceed
- *James 4:7* Resist the Devil

Study Questions for Chapter 12: Security in Life Comes from Being God-Centered

1. What factors in Psalm 139 help us feel secure? Name them.

2. Review the promise in Isaiah 46:4 that will enhance our feeling of security.

3. Name some life situations from which many draw their false security. Study the iceberg graphic noticing the physical, mental, psychological, and then spiritual realms of development, and seeing how that bottom realm of the spiritual development needs to be the largest and strongest.

4. As you concentrate on the spiritual realm, give specific reasons to possess security as you search these Scriptures: John 1:12; Colossians 2:10; John 15:16; Philippians 4:13.

5. If you should feel you don't deserve God's security, get familiar with Romans 8:1–2 and write it down.

6. Spend a lot of time digesting what a God-centered life looks like from the chart in this chapter. Rehearse out loud the many aspects of what the God-centered secure life looks like. Ask yourselves if these descriptions are true of you. Do this exercise regularly. (It will take time and honesty.)

7. Write down some new commitments you are making to be all that God has designed for you to be. See Colossians 2:6.

8. What should my life look like to those around me if I say I truly have hope in Jesus? See Psalm 39:7; 1 Timothy 4:10; Ephesians 4:4.

9. Discuss (on paper and in your group) the habit of disciplining yourself away from a continual negative outlook or allowing a fearful mantra to rule if you indeed claim to be secure in Jesus and claim to be God-centered. See Psalm 56:11; Hebrews 2:13.

10. Do your life choices show that you can sing the song, "I Have Decided to Follow Jesus" and it be true? (Sing it if you know it.)

Insecurity Destroys Everything

Insecurity is obviously the absence of security. It is toxic. We first saw this in the garden with Adam and Eve as they displayed the need to hide because of sin. Then we see it going from bad to worse, destroying relationships, marriages, families, and every walk of life. This is a mindset that destroys, so we need to identify how this might be a part of our lives. We've got to set up a prevention program. What does this insecurity really look like?

No resting in God. There seems to be something always wrong with an insecure person—they cannot be comfortable in their own skin because they continually need to prove themselves to feel okay about themselves. They live in a downer mentality where everything seems hopeless. They think they make themselves feel better about themselves when they find fault with you and others. They are depressive without much purpose to live out. These folks have a way of making everybody around them miserable if they don't join their funk. They can't elevate others because they feel it makes them look lower. I'm sure you have plenty of people in mind who fit this description.

It's so unfortunate how these people **run from themselves** by making bad choice after bad choice. A chaotic life pattern rules most every day. Not realizing it, they set themselves up for more of the same every day. Everything is catastrophic. It's hard for them to evaluate any-thing because they are **blind to themselves**. When you cannot see, you just **keep committing the same disasters** affecting you and others.

As you think over this concept of insecurity and become aware of this force of evil, I pray you will be motivated to put up the mental stop

Decide to stop the chaos

sign to make huge changes in your life. It will be so ful-filling to be able to relax in life with these changes as you initiate your positive life choices. It will make life easier for those around you for sure.

Insecurity shows itself when one's mindset is tainted with unresolved issues in their life. Then, unsettled patterns continue to surface in other relationships and situations. Their unfounded harsh responses to other people leave observers wondering what has just hap-pened with the bazaar reactions observed. Our mindsets are observ-able through our actions. Things can get blown all out of proportion when there are hurts and resentments left unaddressed. Newly targeted people are taking barbs as anger rages within the insecure person. It's so difficult to observe the unfortunate inadequacies of these insecure people promoting damage to those around.

When playing a city league tennis match with a prominent club, my partner and I were in a third set 10-point tie breaker, with our being ahead 8–3. I made a call on the ball to my side, which my part-ner agreed with regarding it being out of bounds. (I do not cheat.) The opponents came unglued and verbally bashed us and then walked off the court, having not finished the match. Unbelievable! I've never seen that done before. We didn't do anything wrong, and they were more than poor sports; they most likely had other issues in life and this was a new target.

We often don't see ourselves because we literally are wearing psy-chological blinders. We do not have a clue how bad off we are. We can be that outwardly beautiful person, with the incredible body, possessing lavish personal possessions with many privileges in life. We can be very "book-learning smart" and making lots of money but somehow be void of a foundational platform of being secure. Oh, that we would get the blinders off! They are causing us and those around much despair. Let's really see what is happening and then put up that stop sign to be and live a different way.

No excuses will be allowed such as, "That's just the way I grew up." Instead, you CAN change; it's a choice. Jesus healed the blind man from birth in John 9. In verse 25 the man says, "one thing I do know, that though I was blind, now I see." Then with spiritual truths we're told how darkness blinds our eyes. That is what insecurity does; we're blind to it. Gratefully, we can go from blind to seeing spiritually as well. We have a big God who can do all things.

Troubled, insecure people will work at covering their inabilities or weaknesses. They must look good in order to feel good about themselves. They'll try and distract from a real situation through joking or laughing about something. Maybe they change the subject. They'll put you down so as to feel better about themselves. Maybe their tactics are with intimidations or mocking or misrepresenting you so their way looks right and best.

Maybe they show their unacceptance by excluding others to assure their superiority would show. They like to take credit for everything because anything less would shine a lesser light for themselves. And of course, they want to point out how something is *your* mistake and not possibly theirs. (You probably roll your eyes in response, either physically or mentally.)

Because hard things are not easily resolved, they cannot deal with hardship or realities very well. They just want to ignore or somehow downplay them. Insecure people are continually striving because somehow they have to be better in order to feel secure. Making many excuses is frequently part of their world.

There are holes in their hearts and, unfortunately, they try all kinds of pleasures to try and make things right. It's hard to have strong, loving relationships because they need to disrupt things with what they think are spiritual patches. They are so busy defending themselves they can't just enjoy being with people. It's a heart thing and only resting in God is going to provide a calm to their rough waters in life. They are running hard from that, because they are simply unsettled.

Their mindset displays a need to fail because that is what is normal or comfortable from their past. They would never admit that. Maybe that's how they grew up. Maybe that's how they have learned to do life. Inferiority plagues their minds, being inadequate, even when they are extremely talented. Such thinking is so opposite to all God has told us in His Word. We don't need an upgrade or to make replacements to proceed productively.

The insecure person needs to portray themselves as superior and insist on always being right while everybody around is wrong. They'll argue, and at all different levels. They are not open for suggestions; they can't listen. They operate against the rules, as they think rules don't apply to them. They make demands of others and insist it be done now, on their terms. Others close at hand become targets of this insecurity. Like we said, this is destructive. "Confidence is silent. Insecurities are loud."[1]

People like this can drive us crazy because they need so much attention. It's important to them that everybody should be "making a fuss" over them and honoring them. They need everybody to be noticing everything they do as they feel they deserve being singled out. This scenario doesn't do well in marriages because they keep acting like they deserve better options, so this kind of person will frequently choose to move on to find somebody else who might do more for them.

These folks simply cannot have fun in life. They need to make everybody around them miserable. They can't bring themselves to change that pattern. Being around them is tense because nobody can be comfortable. The secure person feels obligated to just do what the troubled person wants, to keep the peace.

Unfortunately, it's possible for a split personality to surface. They are somewhat aware their behavior is not acceptable, so they know how to put on a façade. It can look wonderful for a while, but those who are used to their ways know it changes quickly. The one side is incredibly winsome where everybody is impressed how wonderful they are and then the other side comes alive when they are with the people who are closest.

Because they are not living in a comfort zone, they can be intolerant over little and big things. They are discontent, looking for flaws. It's easy for the insecure person to want to make other people look incapable or inefficient. They give them no credibility to make things happen, because they personally need the attention to go to them. There are huge fears of their looking inferior.

The undesirable qualities go on—misrepresenting the truth. Maybe it's exaggerating, undermining, or just not telling it like it is. The story of some description needs to make them look better somehow. Are we seeing how this is a sickness destroying everything in the path? "Arrogance is the camouflage of insecurity."[2]

In the Bible we read about the fruit of the spirit in Galatians 5:22–23, "The fruit of the spirit is love, joy, peace, patience, kindness, goodness, faithfulness, gentleness, self-control." Unfortunately, someone who is plagued with insecurity has a hard time growing this kind of fruit.

We don't have to look very far to see how spouses have abandoned each other or a parent has abandoned their children. And, it's at epidemic level of children abandoning relationship with their parents, as well, as they wish to blame the parents for all of their problems. It's not a pretty picture. Spouses, children and parents are left devastated. Children have the example to go and do likewise as they grow up and have families of their own. The old self-serving quality heads the list and we have a world of very troubled people because of it. *Me first. I need to get what I want and deserve.* We'll look at the further destructive patterns like this in the next chapter. These are definitely mindsets we'd best run away from if we don't want lives to be destroyed.

Self-protection is present in this person. Harming others is a part of their world. If you're insecure, you have a secular view of everything. They see themselves as the center of their own world, that there is no higher authority. They don't want to answer to anyone. They see themselves as higher than God, because that is the highest purpose in a misguided life. That is secular humanism and it colors everything. People can just wait for them because whatever they are doing or thinking is more important than what another does or thinks.

I can't be the problem, they think. *It's the other person.* Blame and shame are their callings. *It's my parents' fault. It's my mate's fault. It's my boss's fault. It's my neighbor's fault. It's my church's fault. I didn't have anything to do with the problem.* We have some real strong evaluating to do with all this. Assessing everybody else's issues is not our job. The entire human race needs to take a class on what blame and shame looks like so we are not so stained in our daily interactions everywhere.

We've already studied the reflections of the secure person, but it's important we really understand what the other side looks like so we can run from it. We'll be more ready to put up that stop sign. Perhaps these might be descriptions of our own life which need to be drastically changed and now. Spend time considering these pages so you can get honest with yourself to understand this reality. It is obvious that many don't understand themselves so whatever their evaluations of others happen to be comes through clouded lenses. This is stressful for observers.

Are you one of those people who expects everybody to jump at your wishes? Do you feel others can't really do enough to please you? What else can they do for you, instead of what might you do for them? Is your conversation with them all about you and your life or do you ask them about what is happening for them? Do you get them talking or is everything all about you (your day, your stories, your plans, your interests, your ideas, your friends or family?) Because these people don't know how to deal with themselves, we find weird things coming out of their mouths that don't have much to do with anything.

The insecure person doesn't allow for differences in people. They probably don't understand the God-designed differences between men and women so they demand and expect others to be like them. They can't rest with people who aren't as gifted as they are or think another way. Others make decisions differently than they do and that isn't tolerated because their way is the only way, they think. They will even get angry over it to demand sameness to their way.

Let's look at Scripture to see the contrast again from the insecure self-serving person to the secure God-serving person. See these qualities as they change from the gravity-pulling arrow down on the right, to the

Being self-centered displays insecurities

- Ultimate Control
- Perfection Demanded
- Do what I say or else
- Dominates
- Threatens
- Demands
- Expects

- Self protects
- Compensates
- Distracts from issue
- Denial/wears blinders
- Shuns truth/correction, suggestions
- Split personality
- Elevates self
- Monopolizes
- Manipulates

- Unrest, Uncomfortable
- Unsettled, Nervous
- Negative, Antsy
- More than grumpy
- Sadness, Sorrow
- Unhappiness
- Doom & Gloom
- Ongoing frustration
- Personal discontent

- Angry
- Mad
- Hostile
- Aggitated/Irritated
- Jealous
- Bitter

REFLECTING

SELF CENTERED

NATURAL BEND

EXPRESSIONS INSECURITIES

- Pokes
- Intimidates
- Mocks
- Insults/Put downs
- Unkind
- Unthoughtful
- Picks away/Nagging
- Name calling
- Correcting/Interrupting
- Undercuts
- Focus on everything negative
- Pushes
- Belittles, Derogatory
- Humiliates
- Demeaning

- Unrelenting takedowns
- Dismantles, keeps chipping (chopping)
- Batters:
  o emotionally
  o mentally
  o psychological
- Extreme repetitive disapproval

- Retaliates
- Blasts
- Overrides
- Betrays

- Fearful
- Suspicious
- Distrustful
- Extreme Questioning
- Doubtful

- Blames
- Accuses
- Finds all faults to point to
- Points attention to others' issues, problems, inadequacies
- Turns issues away from self

- Defends
- Excuses
- Argue
- Has to win, be right, overcome, appear superior
- Tell you black is white
- Lays conditions

- Withdraws
- Excludes
- Walks off
- Hides
- Isolates
- Diverts attention
- Covers over
- Replaces

- Abandons
- Rejects
- Withhold privilege, info, opportunities
- Thwarts (stops process, denies access, just saying no)
- Proceeds without the other

"box of change" in turning the wheel in a different direction, toward pleasing God.

The Secure, God-Serving Person		The Insecure Self
James 1	Considering it joy with trials	Doubting, being like the surf
	Testing producing endurance	of the sea tossed by the wind
	Perseveres under trial	Double-minded, unstable in all his ways
		Carried away and enticed by his own lust
	Quick to hear, slow to speak and anger	
	Ridding yourselves of filthiness	
	Receiving the word implanted	
	Prove yourselves doers of the word	
	Keeping one's self unstained by the world	
James 4	God gives grace to the humble	Quarrels and conflicts
	Submitting to God	Pleasures waging war in your body
	Resisting the devil	Lusting and not having
	Drawing near to God and	Fighting and quarrelling
	Him drawing near to you	Don't ask God so you don't have
	Cleansing your hands toward God	Friendship with the world, hostility
	Purifying your hearts	Boasting in one's arrogance
	Humbling yourself	Knowing right but not doing it (sin)
	The Spirit dwelling in us	Hostility toward God

You cannot exhaust the Scriptures on this topic. The important piece is to become aware of these two opposite descriptions and make sure we put up that mental stop sign to the horribly negative trend we're born with—that sin nature—and make the major change to please our Maker.

Let's look at how the Bible says it again. Second Timothy 3:1–5 spells it out strongly:

> But realize this, that in the last days difficult times will come. For people will be lovers of self, lovers of money, boastful, arrogant, slanderers, disobedient to parents, ungrateful, unholy, unloving, irreconcilable, malicious gossips, without self-control, brutal, haters of good, treacherous, reckless, conceited, lovers of pleasure rather than lovers of God, holding to a form of godliness, although they have denied its power; avoid such people as these."

We'd best establish some careful boundaries or that old sin nature with all of this insecurity can too easily take over our good lives and God's intentions. God is grieved when we allow such choices. And, there are consequences.

The Lord warned us about fear throughout Scripture, so we'd best be aware how our fears and insecurity destroy our productivity. How very little can be done under the spirit of fear. Therefore, let's trust God and not fear, through the power of the Holy Spirit.

The next chapter deals with understanding victimhood, narcissism, and entitlement—issues that are entirely too prevalent in our world. Let's be fully aware of this strong draw and how we may possibly be living this way without even realizing it. Then let's determine to run hard in a new direction.

Study Questions for Chapter 13: Insecurity Destroys Everything

1. What is it that stops an insecure trend so we can feel SAFE? See Proverbs 3:5–6.

2. Why do you think the concept of fear is noted hundreds of times in Scripture?

3. Do we allow our minds to create lies about God's ability to be and do all, and our ability THROUGH Him to overcome? See Colossians 2:8; Ephesians 6:10–12.

4. Do we place our hope for security, rest, and peace in our circumstances, or do we rest in the Lord? See Psalm 37:7; Jeremiah 6:16; Job 11:17–19.

5. Study the chart "Being self-centered displays insecurity." If you see yourself at all, make a private list of changes you would ask God to help you make. Spend time identifying your insecure possible trends.

6. Of the many manifestations of insecurity on the chart describing this negative quality, make a list of the twenty or more least desirable traits shown there driving you crazy about other people, and possibly in yourself. Take time to identify these problems so you can more easily reject their presence in your life.

7. Look at James 1. Make a list of insecure behaviors noted. Then again, do this with James 4. As desired, ask your group to pray for you in helping to stop behaviors of insecurity.

8. Read 2 Timothy 3:1–5 and list those qualities we want to avoid. Ask for accountability in making boundaries to disallow them to rule.

9. Do you realize how obnoxious these insecure traits are that we allow into our lives, as people observe our infantile behaviors? They are not a pretty picture, yet we do have powers to change. Pray with your group that you would utilize these powers to release this insecurity stronghold. See Psalm 9:9.

10. Discuss fear versus trusting God. Offer Scriptures to back this up.

14

Understanding Victimhood, Narcissism, and Entitlement

These three states of mind indeed show a mindset of concentrating on one's SELF and what they want, need or demand. It's all about them—these folks are quite hung up on themselves. It's a continuation of the subject of insecurity which we've just addressed but has a little different twist for each. Ask yourself if these qualities could describe you, because that choice is forever there—clinging to God's master design of purpose or displaying the natural reality of emptiness which fights for purpose.

Victimhood

"Woe is me" is an attitude of victimhood we often see. So many have father or mother wounds from their childhood that display extensive dysfunctions in their family or professional lives later. They take out their deep wounds on others in their immediate spheres with their actions being either active or passive. They seem to have no idea that those early hurts are causing such horrific disruptions, while now blaming many in their close wake for all their troubles.

They feel so crushed from childhood **unknowingly** and are still living it all out, trying to prove themselves to be somebody important. They crawl into a shell in this pain yet hurt those who are close in trying to fix their pain. The hard part is that even brilliant, educated, "success-ful" people fall into this category and those in their wake wonder how such dysfunction could really be possible.

Beyond possible father or mother wounds, numerous former intense life dysfunctions can present a platform for these people to assume that other people's wrong choices are destroying them. Their "normal" stance insists that they are to assume that other people's wrong choices are their problem totally. Yet, other people's mistakes don't demand our poor responses, even through unfortunate happenings.

Justifying self displays huge needs to control life by personally needing to rise above others after encountering real or felt hardships. Really, FELT hardships stimulate the **interpretations** of **assumptions** that these "victims" have wrongfully been viewed and threatened. Do we see an almost sadistic desire to magnify personal rights while refus-ing any personal responsibility to respond well and insisting on destroy-ing others.

To help identify this scenario, what do we observe in many victims?

- the need to look superior as they believe they are superior
- subtly and overtly lie if need be to persuade
- remain angry, obsessed, unforgiving, withholding_____ (fill in the blank)
- pursue revenge to get even
- threaten, hurt, damage, cripple, or maybe sue legally
- refuse to let go or make progress
- hate, stop others with animosity
- insist on destruction, refusal to change
- continue an unhappy trend and sway others that direction
- act with a grade school mentality, proving oneself continually
- provide umpteen reasons why they are totally right
- blame incessantly with one-sided judging
- break normal rules/covenants of God's intentions

Because this syndrome of victimhood is so prevalent, it can be help-ful in this chapter to repeat the reality of this obnoxious trait in various ways so we catch the message and grasp the importance of changing a trend we might possess. May we catch the drift so we see ourselves in reality and do ourselves and everybody around us the favor of displaying a productive way of life, void of victimhood.

Victimhood can go from bad to worse as seen in criminal offenders who don't know how to reasonably handle life's frustrations. Let's curb that option—the goal is to identify this issue and STOP it now.

There are legitimate victims in many situations, such as having been rammed by another car. You were hurt and your car was damaged—you were a victim of theirs. They did cause it and you are cheated out of the use of your personal property and out of a normal body. You may have experienced a fire, earthquake, robbery, devastating illness, and so much more in your life. All of these are huge. You are left stunned and mortified with grief as a victim.

There are many other kinds of victims, whether war victims with injury or death, or sexual abuse. Some have been sued by another becoming a victim of their pursuit to get you to pay. Maybe you've been a victim of workplace injustice where you lost your job to unfair assessments by the boss, and maybe at the hand of dishonest fellow employees. Marriages have broken up and one spouse becomes the victim of the other's dysfunction. Children are left without both parents, being abandoned, and they are victims of wrong-doing. Maybe you're a victim of somebody's misplaced confidence for various reasons.

Then there is more. How is this victimhood defining you? We've all been around many people who INTERPRET everything they hear to be against them. Nothing is fair in their estimation. They think they are always the one who gets the short end of a deal, a decision, whatever. They complain about everything because nothing sets right—they are victims, they think. They feel their life will never work. They got a difficult assignment at their job, at school or at home, because they think everybody has it better than they do.

They think they'll never make it with anything. Nothing is fair, and everybody around has to keep hearing about it. They can't seem to handle not having everything go their way. Their mindset is definitely avoiding to overcome. It's a tool of the devil himself. First Peter 5:8–9 reminds us, "Be of sober spirit, be on the alert. Your adversary, the devil, prowls around like a roaring lion, seeking someone to devour. So resist him, firm in your faith." He'll tell you that you are a victim and not good enough.

The seemingly victim personality frequently remains angry. They feel there's something wrong with everybody and everything, which makes them distrust everybody. Nothing is enough, whether it be attention, time, money, or whatever. They need more, and those around them aren't giving them what they think they deserve. They are victims. So they go about trying to control things because they don't like being left the victim.

They are big on self-protection—so unwilling to give of themselves, to include others, reach out or receive because they're more comfortable staying a victim. They are often withdrawn or depressed. Their negative outlook drives people around them crazy. They keep displaying: sarcasm, intimidation, blackmail, threats, manipulation, pity parties, domination, contradictions, interruptions, nervousness, and the like. It's not a pretty picture being a victim.

They figure the reason they lost an election, a privilege, a friend, a spot on the team, an investment profit is because of others—they feel they are victims of so many others. The victim repeats these lines: "This always happens to me, never to anybody else. Why do I always get taken advantage of? It's just not fair . . ." Their friends and family get tired of hearing the continual sadness and blaming of others they feel in their soul and mind.

The attitudes and comments just don't quit: "Why did you reject me when I was clearly the best choice? You are clearly not doing me justice. Nobody helps me. They have blown it for me." The self-focus goes on, "I never get invited; they leave me out intentionally. They seem to forget me or just ignore that I exist." There is such an unconscious need to fail, be excluded or things go wrong at every juncture.

"I don't deserve this maltreatment. *What about me*? I should have had a major place in this company by now, as I was the best choice," the victim keeps saying, "My glass will always be half empty, never full."

Family, friends and co-workers will feel the identification as we keep expressing how the victim responds to life, and will appreciate that others know what they are observing and living with. The victim lines keep happening. "Nothing is fair." Their intimidations toward others communicate that they feel that others made them experience their bad circumstances.

We all have our moments when things aren't working well—and that's normal. Even the psalmist expresses his frustrations in Psalm 69:20, "Disgrace has broken my heart, and I am so sick. And I waited for sympathy, but there was none, And for comforters, but I found none." The big subject is what we do with this mentality. Do we let it just go on or do we make the necessary changes and go a different direction? Hopefully the latter.

The victim feels so justified because they aren't wrong; it's the other guy. They deserve to have. They are aloof to the facts because they just know what they want and deserve. They've been cheated, they think. They hate being other people's puppets. They camp on all the negatives. They continue to feel they have to take care of themselves because they think nobody else will. It's "poor me" repeatedly. Blah, Blah, Blah. And the observers respond by saying, "the poor baby." So much of this comes from a life of fear—fear that you're not all that you want to be. Isaiah 41:10 gives us His promise with our responsibility, "Do not fear, for I am with you; Do not be afraid, for I am your God. I will strengthen you, I will also help you. I will also uphold you with My righteous right hand."

Our culture is demonstrating another avenue of victimhood. Some students feel uncomfortable or guilty because they felt offended by some teaching they thought was politically incorrect. They believe they are victims. One university president proclaimed to his students, "This is not a day care. It's a university." Any time their feelings are hurt, they feel they are victims. It's interesting how the conscience is involved here. Listen to some strong words from the Oklahoma Wesleyan president, Everett Piper, "Oklahoma Wesleyan is not a "safe place," but rather, a place to learn: to learn that life isn't about you, but about others; that the bad feeling you have while listening to a sermon is called guilt. . . . This is a place where you will quickly learn that you need to grow up."[1]

What are some of the consequences of a victim mentality?

- You stay at an emotional distance from many people.
- Your friendships are temporary.

- You need to get your way regardless of bad responses.
- Your conscience can be blinded. (You don't even know you have a problem.)
- You feel you have rights that aren't being allowed.
- You are angry, sometimes against those who are in a position to help. You don't even realize you have anger.
- You feel the need to get even with people.
- Sometimes your pain is associated with something that happened earlier in your life.
- You may not feel comfortable entering into your kids' childhood because you are not resolved with things that weren't good in your own.
- You doubt your own abilities and lack self-confidence.
- You refuse to turn the wheel and go toward God's design. Pressure keeps pushing you, and you keep copping out and not owning your "stuff."
- You revert to childlike behaviors as people observe you and are embarrassed for you.
- You keep running away from responsibility, because you are a victim.

The answer to this type of thinking stays the same—you take it to the cross. No more paralyzing allowed by the devil. This person, the victim, is probably a hurting person and is crying for help unknowingly. When you have a big God, He takes the burdens and redirects your thoughts. Rehearse the God-factors with His unending character to claim for yourself. DIVERT from the Satan's ways and all the destruction he brings. No more buying the devil's lies. No more playing the victim card. Sing that song, "Leave Your Heavy Burden at the Cross"[2] Only Jesus has the living water to quench your thirst. We are in a battle for the heart and soul, and you can be a winner.

Going free will require choosing: redemption, focusing on hope, restoration, transformation, forgiveness, newness, renewal, surrender, seeking higher ground, the Waymaker, and Promise Keeper, Healer, Miracle Maker, and going from darkness to the light. YOU CAN DO IT—WITH GOD'S HELP.

Be thankful instead of malcontent. Concentrate on virtues as opposed to shortcomings. Recalculate it all. Let your freedom in Christ take you to new levels of joy as you break free from the strongholds of victimhood. Jeremiah 33:6 says, "Behold, I am going to bring to it health and a remedy, and I will heal then; and I will reveal to them an abundance of peace and truth."

Narcissism

Motivational speaker Rick Rigsby waxes eloquent when he says, "Ego is the anesthesia that deadens the pain of stupidity."[3]

There are people in our realms who exude that feeling of *Look at me*. You can almost hear them thinking, *Aren't I something?!* They may not say it but they are thinking, *Don't you wish you could be just like me or have all that I have?* They don't realize how childishly immature they appear. Proverbs 16:18–19 speaks to this condition, "Pride goes before destruction, And a haughty spirit before stumbling. It is better to be of a humble spirit with the needy, Than to divide the spoils with the proud."

That superiority complex-mindset shows up in most circles. These people think they actually are God. It's quite sad watching wealthy adults with this description acting like grade-schoolers. They can act so pious, thinking their earthly goods make them better than others and treating them as sub-standard.

"The selfish road leads us to walk alone, pursuing all we can gather into our arms. The godly road leads us to walk with and care for others and to walk with God. In doing so, we find all the peace and fulfillment that others grab for in vain."[4] It's not a pretty picture observing folks on the selfish road instead of the path designed by our Creator.

Let's look at the dictionary definition of a narcissist: "A person who is overly self-involved, and often vain and selfish. A person who suffers from narcissism, deriving erotic gratification from admiration of their own physical or mental attributes."[5]

By definition, this person is in need of a lot of attention. They display excessive self-love. They are so insecure that they have this huge need to magnify themselves and in turn, treating people in their path

as someone who needs to do things their way or get out of the way.
They go to extreme measures to push their way around. The pleasures,
suggestions, and rights of those around do not matter to this person.
They feel power in telling people "no"—no other ideas will not be
accepted.

Why is it so important that we talk about narcissism? It's a destructive mindset that harms those in its wake. And as we gain awareness
of it—possibly seeing it in ourselves—we'll be more prone to go a different direction. Very often, the person with this mindset cannot see
themselves.

The Bible speaks to the issue: "People who trusted in themselves
that they were righteous, and viewed others with contempt. . . . Everyone who exalts himself will be humbled, but the one who humbles
himself will be exalted" (Luke 18:9, 14).

We're born with that gravity pull of self-orientation. We can be
saved from the PENALTY of sin when accepting Jesus into our lives
to replace that sin we were born with as we ask for forgiveness. Then,
moment by moment we can be saved by the POWER of sin as we
choose to access that power through prayer. Someday when we get to
heaven we are saved from the PRESENCE of sin—glorious day!

We aren't robots and get to choose. How do I choose to think? How
do I choose to act? How do I choose to view myself? Scripture always
gives us the path to the good life. Romans 12:3 says, "not to think more
highly of himself than he ought to think; but to think so as to have
sound judgment." Second Corinthians 3:5–6 gives further instruction
as to how we should see ourselves: "Not that we are adequate in ourselves so as to consider anything as having come from ourselves, but
our adequacy is from God, who also made us adequate." How am I
choosing to live life?

Do the following traits describe someone close to you—or possibly
even yourself? The narcissist sees only what they want regardless of what
YOU might like, need, or want. Again, their way is more important
regardless of how it might inconvenience you, hurt you, disappoint
you, or be wrong. Things need to go their way, or others around will
usually pay. They feel obligated to intimidate, mock, or undermine to
get what they demand. They are bossy and not tolerant with ways other

than theirs. *Everything is about them.* They see themselves as superior. They need extensive admiration, so they will "work a crowd" to dominate and look the best.

Being a narcissist is not limited to being either a man or a woman; the reality exists in either sex. For a moment here, I'll speak to an attitude prevalent in a growing number of women. Some are not appreciating the God directive that future generations be born, as God says in Genesis 1:28, "Be fruitful and multiply, and fill the earth, and subdue it." Then, in Proverbs 22:6 we're told, "Train up a child in the way he should go." So when I read about ladies saying, "I need my time, money, and decisions to benefit myself because I love my life, not being burdened by the lack of freedom with having children," I am troubled with such self-orientation. The mindset of "I love doing what I want, when I want, to make me happy" demonstrates the life of an individual over God's plan.

Narcissists demand space, privilege, money spent their way and time given to them for whatever they want in every realm. They feel they deserve more of whatever. Have you been to a dinner where this kind of a person took more food than was appropriate when a larger number of people needed to be fed? They have no concept of other people's needs. It doesn't bother them to be rude and inconsiderate, while others stand back and are appalled at the arrogance shown. A narcissist needs to make others feel ashamed or insecure and question themselves. The victim of a narcissist begins to wonder if they are losing their minds being used as pawns. This technique is called "gaslighting," where the abuser causes others to doubt their sanity.

For the narcissist there is little room in relationships with other people who present a threat for approval. The attention must go to themselves and thus the other person is forced to have no contribution. Their strengths and worth are not accepted. The need to control or dominate assures their ego to remain superior. You could say there is not room in a relationship for the narcissist and another—it has to be all about them.

Their grandiose sense of self-importance literally sickens people around them. They seem to live in a fantasy world with delusions of grandeur. This is a mental condition. How is narcissistic personality disorder (NPD) described? They are "in love with an idealized, grandiose image of themselves. And they're in love with this inflated self-image precisely because it allows them to avoid deep feelings of insecurity."[6] Working with other people in relationships shows a demand for compliance.

"People with NPD are those who are preoccupied with their own success and with a grand sense of self-importance that influences their decision-making and interactions."[7] I'm sure you are thinking right now of people with this description. Whether it's decisions at the business or home, they are obvious. There's no room for your ideas, your stuff, your way to order your closet, your ideas of who your guests are, or how you spend your time—the narcissist rules.

It surfaces from our sin nature, of course. Sometimes the sins of the generations get passed down where childhood abuse, traumas, or neglect could be factors. Did a parent place perfectionistic demands on them? Was a parent smothering a child with unrealistic pampering? What are they trying to prove? Do they put their child under a spell of domination or infatuation? Whatever the stimulus to encourage one toward extreme self-focus in defending themselves, this person can redye the fabric of the heart and make a change as they realize what they are really like.

God wants the better way for you. Second Peter 2 speaks the heart of God and His desires to keep these wayward people from "suffering wrong as the wages of doing wrong" (v. 13). The description of these are as follows, "those who indulge the flesh in its corrupt passion, and despise authority. Reckless, self-centered, they speak abusively . . ." (v. 10). Further description to include those self-willed people is this, "abandoning the right way, they have gone astray" (v. 15). Verse 19 continues, "for by what anyone is overcome, by this he is enslaved." If you are entangled in this chosen demise, you are "turn[ing] away from the holy commandment " (v. 21). This is a huge consideration for us to mull over.

Thomas Sowell says this of the narcissist, "Some of the biggest cases of mistaken identity are among intellectuals who have trouble remembering that they are not God."[8]

Entitlement

This is a day and age when the subject of a person's rights is a big topic. More and more people think they have rights for whatever and feel they are due privileges whether they have earned them or deserve them. It doesn't matter that others have worked for what they have. Some kids feel that the parents need to give them pretty much everything. They don't want to work for them; they feel they are owed it all. We could call it greed. The government has added to this mindset with so many handouts. People expect to be given this, that, and everything.

Consider this assessment from an incredible, brilliant Black man who grew up in Harlem, served in the Marine Corps during the Korean War, graduated Magna Cum Laude from Harvard, has a Masters from Columbia, is an economist, social theorist, philosopher, author, Senior Fellow Hoover Institution member, Stanford University, has the National Humanities Medal and Francis Boyer award, "One of the consequences of such notions as 'entitlements' is that people who have contributed nothing to society feel that society owes them something, apparently just for being nice enough to grace us with their presence."[9]

Back to the Bible again, 2 Thessalonians 3:10 says, "if anyone is not willing to work, then he is not to eat either." The book of Proverbs describes the sluggard, "His hands refuse to work" (21:25). "One who works his land will have plenty of food, But one who follows empty pursuits will have plenty of poverty. A faithful person will abound with blessings" (28:19–20).

It used to be that kids on sports teams would receive a trophy when they won a tournament, a league play-off game, or some finale. Things have changed and now every team player who participates gets a trophy, no matter if their team won or not.

What about meals at school? Nobody use to be fed breakfasts or lunches at school, but things have changed. People feel entitled. Maybe it's about grades in school where you expect the high mark when you didn't work to deserve it. Then, at graduation time you might get a diploma now after not getting the grades or having taken the number of classes that use to be expected. Is this description of behavior being observed more and more?

Feeling entitled without being responsible to have earned something is a mindset that displays arrogance. Such a profile is indeed not what we want to own if we want to be a God-follower. Blessings on you as you work to identify whether you've allowed any of these three aspects of self to define your life, and then to actively take steps to divert from them to the unselfish lifestyle, God's better way.

Oh that we would be aware how the devil places a deep need within us to be a self-oriented person. Paul writes to the church at Colosse wanting "to see your good discipline and the stability of your faith in Christ" (Col. 2:5 NASB95). May we be INTENTIONAL with our work to disallow ourselves to be caught up in victimhood, narcissism and entitlement. How? "If you have been raised with Christ, **keep seeking the things that are above**, where Christ is, seated at the right hand of God. **Set your mind** on the things that are above, not on the things that are on earth" (Col. 3:1–2).

Years ago I was on a thirty-seven concerts choir tour in Southern California and I remember a great plaque placed behind a pulpit in a big church which said, "Sir, we would see Jesus." Such a good reminder to anyone whose life was represented before those people. May any scales present on our eyes fall so we can see the need to live free of the entanglement that would display victimhood, narcissism or entitlement to a world in our sphere.

Hmm, could this be me?

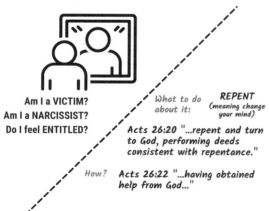

Am I a VICTIM?
Am I a NARCISSIST?
Do I feel ENTITLED?

What to do about it:

REPENT
(meaning change your mind)

Acts 26:20 "...repent and turn to God, performing deeds consistent with repentance."

How?   **Acts 26:22** "...having obtained help from God..."

Consider the words in the devotional by Paul David Tripp, *New Morning Mercies*, "You have only two choices: an "on earth" way of thinking... this right here, right now physical moment, or an "above" way of thinking that looks at life from the vantage point of the grand redemptive story and, more specifically, from the perspective of the person and work of the Lord Jesus Christ?"[10] May you go for the heavenly mindset!!

Study Questions for Chapter 14: Understanding Victimhood, Narcissism, and Entitlement

1. Look up the meaning of these three words and ponder how anti-God they are.

2. Consider how opposite the "woe is me" syndrome is to the divine nature of being others-oriented. Read 2 Peter 1:2–10. Verse 9 describes the person as _____ if they've forgotten their divine nature. Therefore, what is the admonition in verse 10 to counteract that unfruitful self-focus? Peter knew the human tendency so he said he wanted to "stir you up by way of reminder" (v. 13).

3. Discuss our Christian responsibility to forgive—avoiding the victim mentality "so that no advantage would be taken of us by Satan, for we are not ignorant of his schemes" (2 Cor. 2:11). Read Ephesians 4:32 and 2 Corinthians 2:8–11. List various damages incurred when unrepentant forgiveness does not take place, whether you were wronged or not. Share your victories with this. Commit to forgiving in your life and ask for prayers regarding this.

4. How have you seen victimhood played out in your circles? Narcissism? Entitlement?

5. Discuss the Christian's privilege and responsibility to honor God with their life as opposed to demanding their self-focus on everything.

6. How can we counteract blatant displays of self as we observe others in our spheres? Suggest some (artwork) lines to use with people that might help them see themselves without overly offending them (carefully chosen words for a beautiful finish).

7. How are these self-seekers described in Luke 18:9 and 14?

8. Read 2 Corinthians 3:5–6. Are we adequate in ourselves? Where is our adequacy?

9. What does the Bible clearly say about how to think accurately? See Romans 12:3.

10. What does the Bible say about being responsible to work? See 2 Thessalonians 3:10; Proverbs 21:25; 28:19.

11. How should we think about the three subjects of this chapter? See Colossians 3:1–2. Pray for our friends who are swept into these very unfortunate patterns.

Making Smart Choices
with God's Mindset

If our flashlight batteries are weak, we change them for a brighter light. In this "game" of life, there are basic rules we need follow for the kind of conclusion we wish to accomplish.

We possess the ability to make choices and keep our minds from the paths of destruction. With the many forces surrounding us, it's easy for us to fall into the mind control of others if we aren't careful. When we find ourselves in the middle of compromising or destructive developments, we need to learn to divert. That will be what we choose to think about, how we respond mentally, how we spend our time, etc. It's going to be hard work to learn how to divert to paths of productivity and not just fall victim to a troubled path. Be creative in how you'll do something different from going the negative route. Redirect instead of falling victim to sadness. The better way is to put away the old and put on the new.

Our minds control so much of life so we must train our minds to think beyond. The **mindset** determines the **choices** which determine the **consequences**. It's a biblical principle we see in Galatians 6:7–8, "Do not be deceived, God is not mocked; for whatever a person sows, this he will also reap. For the one who sows to his own flesh will reap corruption from the flesh, but the one who sows to the Spirit will reap eternal life from the Spirit."

What kind of seeds are you sowing? Would it be greed and anger or might it be love and kindness with forgiveness? It is your forever choice. (Without it, you are your own prisoner.) What kind of a mindset are your consequences coming from? "God's desire for you is to know where your injuries and deficits are, whether self-induced or other-induced. Ask him to shed light on the significant relationships and forces that have contributed to your own boundary struggles."[1]

Maybe you need help in understanding how your mindset came to be. Consider Psalm 139:23–24, "Search me, God, and know my heart; Put me to the test and know my anxious thoughts; And see if there is any hurtful way in me, And lead me in the everlasting way." There's no better advice than that. If during your evaluations you have discovered some previously hidden issues, it's not too late to make some changes. Only you get to decide your choices.

We feed our minds—the good food and the unhealthy garbage. Are we dwelling on how bad we have it and how so many things have gone against us? Do we tell ourselves how deficient we are and insist on being victims? Do we stay fixed on the negative side of life? Do we feel justified in remaining angry at all those who displayed injustice on our life path? Rather than insisting on living life by the circumstances around us, let's choose the better way! Jesus says, "I am the way, and the truth, and the life" (John 14:6). We're reminded in 1 Samuel 17:47, "The battle is the LORD's."

There is a popular and easy way, but we need to choose God's way. Matthew 7:13 reminds us, "Enter through the narrow gate; for the gate is wide and the way is broad that leads to destruction, and there are many who enter through." Then there is the other route: "For the gate is narrow and the way is constricted that leads to life, and there are few who find it" (v. 14). False prophets will lead us astray, and we'll know them by their fruits. We are told to **guard** the way (Gen. 3:24) and to **commit** our way and **trust** in Him (Ps. 37:5). The WAY we choose is key and will give us a mindset to proceed for the appropriate consequences. Tony Evans tells us, "Others do not control your destiny. God does. Listen to Him—not them."[2]

Developing a productive mindset will be a huge legacy to pass down to the next generation—demonstrating the intentions of our living God. Your children will learn from watching you and how you "do life." Responses and attitudes and covert actions display what is important to you. You are mentors to everybody in your realm—they are watching. Our feelings of worth are activated by Scripture, taking our cues from God to stand tall through it all. Go back and rehearse all those Scriptures in chapter 9 of what God does for you to enhance your feelings of worth and value and care. First Peter 5:7 says, "He cares about you." You matter. Your mindset matters. God's reputation matters. And, all those statutes He gives are "for your good" says Deuteronomy 10:13.

Granted, there are many negatives to deal with in life. And God does need to give his wayward children a "thorn in the flesh" to get their attention sometimes (2 Cor. 12:7). What thorn does it take with us?

You can work through the heart expressions of many saints in the Scriptures who pour out their hearts with the "woe is me" syndrome. They go on and on about how bad things are for them. Depression sets in severely. Their dysfunctional responses display psyche cases and how much of a victim they feel they are. Then, God's truth gets hold of them and they get straight. The lights turn on. Read through Lamentations 3:1–20 and observe the dismay and oppression of feeling so rejected. Then, **the light comes on**: "Great is Your faithfulness. The LORD is my portion."

> I recall this to my mind, Therefore I have hope. The LORD's lovingkindnesses indeed never cease, For His compassions never fail. They are new every morning; Great is Your faithfulness. "The Lord is my portion," says my soul, "Therefore I have hope in Him." The LORD is good to those who wait for Him, To the person who seeks Him. It is good that he waits silently For the salvation of the LORD. (vv. 21–26 NASB95)

That light is going to shine when we finally choose to bow to the authority of our big God—when we choose not to allow ourselves to be distracted by the natural pull downward. James 1:22–25 gives us

From darkness into light

Like the Bible in action...

our instructions, "Prove yourselves doers of the word, and not merely hearers who deceive themselves. For if anyone is a hearer of the word and not a doer, he is like a man who looks at his natural face in a mirror . . . he has immediately forgotten what kind of person he was. But one who has looked . . . and continued in it . . . an active doer, this person will be blessed in what he does." That is what we want—to be blessed in what we do.

Reminder, we've got to get off that gravity track of the old nature and turn the wheel to go another direction. *Divert is the forever life assignment.*

Reviewing the former chapters in this book can help understand why and how to choose the God-ordained path in life. Let's list some helpful ways to run in the right direction:

- Listen to God in His Word, being open to instruction
- Rehearse that you are able because He is able
- Evaluate your focus to allow Lordship to rule; challenge former limits
- Assure your foundation is strong or expect problems
- Plug into your power source: *prayer with God*
- Enjoy how you overcome evil as you walk in the light daily
- Confess your wrongdoing to the Almighty, and make it right, turn from it
- Paddle upstream instead of floating down with the gravity pull downward
- Run to the light, choosing the upright way
- Allow God to be the judge, not you
- Believe you are God's workmanship, no apologizing
- Walk worthy of the gospel
- Avoid self-centeredness
- Display the fruit of the Spirit (refresh yourself what that fruit is)

- Become very aware of the powers that trick you Satan's way
- Divert from obvious ungodly exposures
- Seek building relationships around godly patterns
- Flee quickly from deeds of the flesh
- Think quickly before jumping into bad patterns, controlling your thought life
- Rehearse your heritage of being God's child
- Make WWJD decisions (what would Jesus do)
- Find ways to honor others instead of putting yourself first
- Decide to make a difference in life
- Don't let pettiness be your mantra
- Stop any anxiety tendencies and feel God's promises instead
- Use today productively
- Pursue responsibilities and don't be lazy
- Show gratefulness as opposed to discontentedness
- Be optimistic rather than finding problems everywhere
- Refuse past failures to dominate you
- Spend time with your family
- Don't be a pity-party person
- Be a regular part of a teaching Bible church and support God's people
- Trust and don't fear, letting God do His work
- Submit to God rather than to cultural trends
- Overcome evil with good
- Stand up for the cause of right; fight the good fight
- Choose you this day whom you will serve and let your light shine

Psalm 27:1, 3, "The LORD is my light and my salvation; Whom shall I fear? The LORD is the defense of my life; Whom should I dread? . . . My heart will not fear . . . I am confident." When you choose to let God take you through life, you go from walking in the dark to having your path lightened. And, you have the power. "Greater is He who is in you than he who is in the world." (1 John 4:4). Then my life verse to remember through our process is, "With people this is impossible, but with God all things are possible" (Matt. 19:24).

The cocreator of Chicken Soup for the Soul speaks to success. He says, "People don't understand the power of their own thoughts. Most people are reactive thinkers. The problem is we're drawn to the habit of negative thinking instead of trying new things. I use this metaphor, that if you know the combination to a lock, the lock has to open."[3]

If you want to be successful in anything, you need a positive mind-set—*never give up* as you go over those hurdles in the race of life. If Jesus was betrayed and hung on a cross to die (Luke 22:48; 23:46), why should we think we're above the living God?

In the midst of toxic circumstances, you have two choices—to harbor bitterness or to forgive. The natural response is to insist on holding wrong-doers hostage for a lifetime OR to forgive as Jesus has forgiven us for our iniquities (Eph. 4:32). "Forgiveness does not change the past but it does enlarge the future."[4]

Choosing connectedness helps create empathy, which helps dissolve the lack of bonding. The person who has been full of themselves necessarily displays the lack of smart choices, lacking necessary empathy. Let's get connected and display empathy toward all.

I close with a story. When getting ready for my youngest son's birthday party dinner years ago, I needed to place all five leaves in our table. It really takes two people to close it up correctly, but I was in a hurry and so gave a big nudge with my hip to close the gaps. The table runners and all the leaves crashed to the floor, leaving the table out of commission not only for that party but for some time to come. If I had only got **"smart enough fast enough,"** that damage would never have happened. That phrase is a great reminder for us in our lives ahead. We already have the design plan, the tools, the power—we just need to incorporate our will. "My God will supply *all your needs* according to His riches in glory in Christ Jesus" (Phil. 4:19).

Let's concentrate on all we can BE as opposed to what we can DO or ACCOMPLISH in life. It takes a mindset with the God-factor permeating everything. It is exciting to think that those around us might even be motivated to live a life of excellence because our mindset choices have stopped them in their tracks to rethink what is really important in life. Enjoy the productivity of all your smart choices ahead with your recalculated mindset! Why would we want another way?

Study Questions for Chapter 15: Making Smart Choices with God's Mindset

1. What are the results of different choices of a mindset? See Galatians 6:7.

2. How do I decipher which way to go in life? See Psalm 139:23–24.

3. Do we have help available to make the better choices daily? See John 14:6; 1 Samuel 17:47.

4. What do I need to do in making smart choices? See Josh. 24:14; Psalm 37:5.

5. Many portions of Scripture display the dismay of various characters in the Bible before the light shone on their darkness. See Lamentations 3:21. What were the prophet Jeremiah's various responses when the light covered his darkness?

6. How can I develop confidence in life? See Psalm 27:1, 3.

7. Regardless the experiences and hurdles in life, who is my extreme example? See Luke 22:48.

8. Do you believe 1 John 4:4?

9. What is your resource for feeling equipped to make the best choices in life? See Philippians 4:19.

10. Beyond your primary smart choice of being saved, what is your strong reminder of how to be equipped for every good work in life? Read 2 Timothy 3:14–17. Write out your key blessings from this passage and give thanks!

11. Discuss the need for actively forgiving and why. See Ephesians 4:32.

12. Discuss the relationship between connectedness, empathy, bonding, and smart choices. Offer Scripture passages from your mental file drawers.

Acknowledgments

Thanks to Fidelis Publishing (Gary Terashita and Oliver North) for helping our culture find answers for developing God-oriented mindsets through Scripture by publishing this work. Thank you to Zee Farrouge for his skillful work in creating the graphics throughout the book for the readers' maximum understanding of the concepts communicated. Thanks to my many Bible study friends who have labored over the content of this book with me to assure that the readers receive God's message for knowing how to live after God's heart. To each endorser, I thank you for taking the time to absorb this message and help others to grasp the value of this message for themselves. I also acknowledge you smart readers who are determined to gain God's perspective by studying the principles presented in this book and making necessary life changes for that productive life you indeed wish to live.

Notes

Chapter 1

1. Booker T. Washington quote at https://www.goodreads.com/quotes /83677-success-always-leaves-footprints.

2. V. Raymond Edmond, "The Disciplines of Life, Wheaton, IL, Scripture Press Foundation, 1948, p. 38

Chapter 2

1. Billy Graham, Teen Challenge Southeast Region Orlando, July 26, 2020.

Chapter 3

1. G. K. Chesterton, *The Autobiography of G. K. Chesterton* (San Francisco: Ignatius Press, 2016), 217.

2. Donald Miller, *A Million Miles in a Thousand Years: What I Learned While Editing My Life* (Nashville: Thomas Nelson, 2009), 108.

Chapter 4

1. Isaac Newton, 1675 letter, "Letter from Sir Isaac Newton to Robert Hooke," Historical Society of Pennsylvania. Retrieved June 6, 2018, the concept dated to the twelfth century, according to John of Salisbury and attributed to Bernard of Chartres.

2. Adapted from Watty Piper, *The Little Engine That Could*, a Little Golden Book Classic (New York: Penguin Random House, 1930–2021).

3. Don Moen, "God Will Make a Way," 1992, taken from Isaiah 43:16.

4. Natalie Walters, "Brothers Who Cofounded a $100 Million Company Say This Question Their Mom Asked Every Night at Dinner Is What Inspired Their Business," *Business Insider*, December 17, 2015, https://www.business insider.com/life-is-good-founders-say-this-question-inspired-their-business -2015-12.

5. Sidney E. Cox, "My Lord Knows the Way Through the Wilderness," 1951.

6. Bill and Gloria Gaither, "Because He Lives," October 1971.

7. William DeVaughn, "Oh Be Thankful for the Good Things That You've Got," March 1972.

8. Paul Overstreet, "Dig Another Well," 1989, https://www.youtube.com/watch?v=98yC7gV-gQU.

Chapter 5

1. Booker T. Washington quote, https://quotefancy.com/quote/2360057/Booker-T-Washington-A-lie-doesn-t-become-truth-wrong-doesn-t-become-right-and-evil-doesn.

2. Thomas Sowell, *The Thomas Sowell Reader* (New York: Basic Books, 2011), 402.

3. Brad Lyles, MD, "How Borderline Personality Disorder helps explain the left," Commentary on WND News Center, November 18, 2021, https://www.wnd.com/2021/11/borderline-personality-disorder-helps-explain-left/.

4. Max Lucado, *You'll Get through This: Hope and Help for Your Turbulent Times* (Nashville: Thomas Nelson, 2013), 39; Lucado, *Fearless: Imagine Your Life without Fear* (Nashville: Thomas Nelson, 2009), 74.

Chapter 6

1. C. S. Lewis, *The Problem of Pain* (1940; repr., New York: HarperCollins, 2015), 92.

2. Sarah Hupp, *First Aid for the Spirit* (White Plains, NY: Peter Pauper Press Inc., 2000).

3. Words from Elliette Harrison, wife of Promise Keeper CEO Ken Harrison, Facebook, August 26, 2021.

4. Priscilla Shirer, "Who's Your Daddy," https://www.youtube.com/watch?v=At6pFpb46Sl.

5. "Selected Quotes from Golda Meir," from Gold Meir Center for Political Leadership, https://www.msudenver.edu/golda-meir-center/golda-meir/quotes/.

6. Golda Meir, AZQUOTES.COM, BrainyQuote.com with Golda Meir quotes, http://www.sanvello.com post, and http://lamfearlessouyl.com video (4:52)

Chapter 7

1. "An Important Development in Nanci's Health," Journal entry, August, 31, 2021, https://www.epm.org/updatesnanci/.

2. "Chemo Begins Tomorrow," Journal entry, November 1, 2021, https://www.epm.org/updatesnanci/.

3. Paul Norquist, Facebook post, January 2, 2022.

4. "Your Past Does Dictate Your Future—Elizabeth Smart Inspirational Documentary," YouTube, August 22, 2020, https://www.youtube.com/watch?v=u4acqH73pus.

5. Jay McKinney; CaringBridge; Facebook, July 16, 2020.

6. Janice Bramwell regarding Joel Bramwell; CaringBridge, August 20–27, 2021.

7. Dave Jongeward, CaringBridge, June and July 13, 2021.

8. Katherine Halberstadt Anderson, "For Such a Time," *Under the Tower*, Wheaton College magazine.

9

10. Judy McDermott, "Diana Golden—• Skier on one leg beats most on two and carries that vigor into rest of life," *The Oregonian*.

Chapter 9

1. "He Owns the Cattle on a Thousand Hills" © 1948 by John W. Peterson Music Co.

Chapter 11

1. J. David Branon, "Sharing the Load," *Our Daily Bread*, June 1993, no. 3.

2. Corrie Ten Boom, *I Stand at the Door and Knock: Meditations by the Author of The Hiding Place* (Grand Rapids: Zondervan, 2008), 95.

3. Corrie ten Boom in a letter from China to America's pastors in 1974, "Corrie Ten Boom and the Rapture," https://www.onethingministries.net/resources/articles/corrie-ten-boom-and-the-rapture/.

4. Original source unknown.

5. Brigitte Nicole, as quoted January 3, 2021 in https://tamarakulish.com/2021/01/03/your-journey-will-be-much-lighter-and-easier-if-you-dont-carry-your-past-with-you/.

6. Kelby McNab, Facebook, November 7, 2019, printed with permission, https://www.facebook.com/kelbymcnab/photos/a.143217609852230/520925422081445/?type=3&eid=ARBsFitsrCqHoadtMaaYBMAtDaApFb6LSwX8NWf0jVhYndoC1_LY9-b8wGy6yr8c-K7oRHZIUDcX74I_.

7. Norm Maves Jr. article on Tony Volpentest, *The Oregonian*, May 15, 1991, B1.

8. Katie Frohnmayer, "Katie: Girl loved life despite trials of battling disease," *The Oregonian*, A18 (date unknown).

9. "Helping People Live Courageously, The Power of the Powerless," *The Encourager*, Vol. 1, No. 4 (Spring 1995): 1–2.

10. Rikki Rogers quote, https://www.quotespedia.org/authors/r/rikki-rogers/strength-doesnt-come-from-what-you-can-do-it-comes-from-overcoming-the-things-you-once-thought-you-couldnt-rikki-rogers/.

11. Definition of "divert," https://www.dictionary.com/browse/divert.

12. Booker T. Washington, *Up from Slavery: An Autobiography* (New York: Doubleday, Page & Co., 1907), 39.

Chapter 12

1. http://www.bestonlineengineeringdegree.com/the-10-worst-high-rise-building-collapses-in-history/

2. Brett James and Troy Verges, recorded by American country music artist Jessica Andrews, "Who I Am," released 2001, https://www.youtube.com/watch?v=Jd9zYKLepCw.

Chapter 13

1. Jane Curnow, What Does Low Self Worth Look Like, https://janecurnow.com/2017/05/01/what-does-low-self-worth-look-like/, retrieved Dec. 5, 2022.

2. Tim Fargo quote: https://www.askideas.com/tag/tim-fargo-quotes/.

Chapter 14

1. "University President to Students: 'This Is Not a Day Care,'" CBN News, August 9, 2017, https://www1.cbn.com/cbnnews/us/2017/august/university-president-to-students-this-is-not-a-day-care.

2. "Leave Your Heavy Burdens at the Cross," John. Willard Peterson, born Nov. 1, 1921, died Sept. 20, 2006. Song copyright date unknown.

3. Dr. Rick Rigsby, Cal Maritime Commencement Address 2017, https://thadeusamadeuscom.wordpress.com/2017/10/14/this-dr-rick-rigsby-delivers-quite-possibly-a-top-5-commencement-speech-of-all-time/; Booker T Washington at Goodreads.com and Frank Leahy at quotationspage.com and allauthor.com.

4. Linda Weber, *Mom, You're Incredible* (Colorado Springs: Focus on the Family, 1994), 159.

5. Definition of "narcissist," https://www.dictionary.com/browse/narcissist.

6. Melinda Smith and Lawrence Robinson, "Narcissistic Personality Disorder," updated November 14, 2022, https://www.helpguide.org/articles/mental-disorders/narcissistic-personality-disorder.htm.

7. Jodi Clark, "What Is a Covert Narcissist?" Updated July 20, 2022, https://www.verywellmind.com/understanding-the-covert-narcissist-4584587.

8. Thomas Sowell quote in Jason L. Riley, *Maverick: A Biography of Thomas Sowell* (New York: Hachette, 2021), 123.

9. Thomas Sowell quote, https://minimalistquotes.com/thomas-sowell-quote-4335/.

10. Paul David Trip, *New Morning Mercies: A Daily Gospel Devotional* (Wheaton, IL: Crossway, 2014), July 8.

Chapter 15

1. Dr. Henry Cloud and Dr. John Townsend, *Boundaries: When to Say Yes, How to Say No to Take Control of Your Life* (Grand Rapids: Zondervan, 2017), 62.

2. Tony Evans, Twitter, August 6, 2012, https://twitter.com/drtonyevans/status/232471391390294016.

3. Jack Canfield interview, by Wendy Cole, Realtor Magazine, Dec. 2007, p.48, quoting from his book, The Success Principles, Mariner Books, 10th anniversary now Jan. 27, 2015, co-written with author Janet Switzer.

4. Paul Boese, "Forgiveness," *Quote: The Weekly Digest* 53, no. 8 (February 19, 1967): 146.